ISBN: 9781729429280

Imprint: Independently Published

ACKNOWLEDGEMENTS

First and foremost, I have to acknowledge and give the highest thanks and praise to Jesus Christ! Without him, this book wouldn't exist. I thank God for blessing me with the gift to write, and for the determination and desire to keep writing. I thank God for his word that encouraged me throughout this whole writing process.

Also, I want to appreciate all my family and friends for the great support, understanding and patience towards me on this journey, and for giving me space when I needed it. I appreciate all the prayers as well.

Special thanks, to my big sister-friend Rachel, for taking the lovely photos of me, it's much appreciated. Love you girl!
My gratitude goes towards my coach and mentor – Francisca Payne, from the "Women on a mission Mastermind Group", for praying for me, giving me advice, sharing her expertise as an experienced author herself, and for motivating me throughout this journey. Not forgetting the other ladies in the group who also prayed for me and encouraged me. I'm truly blessed and extremely grateful.

Last but not least, I thank God for YOU! Thank you for choosing to read my book. I pray it blesses you and impacts your life immensely. Amen.

CONTENTS

INTRODUCTION

At the beginning of 2015, the Lord placed it on my heart to write a book specifically for young Christians, encouraging them to be strong in their faith and live a life that's pleasing to Him.

It took me a long time to write this book due to various setbacks, but I thank God that I remained obedient to the call on my life. I feel very humbled and grateful that my Heavenly Father trusted me with this assignment.

It's an incredible feeling to know your purpose and walk in it. This is me walking in my purpose! I'm a 23-year-old woman who has been through certain things. I know that the struggle is REAL sometimes!

Living a Christian life is not always easy. When we go to school, college, university or work etc. we sometimes feel pressured to follow and adapt to the behaviour and lifestyle of our peers.
It is hard because even though we are able to distinguish between right and wrong, as young people, we often desire to be accepted by others. It's understandable; no one enjoys the feeling of being rejected. Rejection hurts!

I've seen how this fear of being a social outcast has caused many young people to turn their back on God. They devote so much time into pleasing others and end up dropping their Godly standards in the process, thereby becoming lovers of the world.
How do you think God feels?

There is a growing trend of young people trying to be everything that they are not. Why can't we just be who God has called us to be?

Many distractions are around, life is getting busier and it seems like we have time for everything else but Jesus Christ. I know Satan is happy about this; he loves to distract us and divert our attention from God. He attacks our minds, feeds us lies, tempts us and deceives us.

Satan's sole purpose, is to prevent us from getting closer to Jesus. He is hell-bent on destroying our purpose and destiny. Why? Because Satan knows the power of Jesus Christ and the power that we obtain through Him. He knows that with God, we have the power to cancel all his plans, dethrone him and tear his kingdom down.

The devil fears us! In this book, I will share some of my own experiences and struggles, and also explain how I overcame trials with God's help. I just want you to know, that I don't have it all together; I've made mistakes, and I'm still making mistakes. I still have moments of weakness but God is working on me, and He can do the same for you if you let Him.

I can guarantee you that this book will be authentic. I'll be dealing with issues that I believe are relatable to young people. I'm confident that from reading this book, you will learn to trust God more, be challenged and moved to step out on faith and desire to have a much deeper relationship with God.

CHAPTER 1

IDENTITY CRISIS

CHAPTER 1

IDENTITY CRISIS

What is identity crisis? Well, an identity crisis is a condition of being unaware of who you really are, where you belong and what your purpose is in life. Your identity is what characterises you.

It consists of your physical appearance, personality, beliefs, hobbies, and interests. Identity also relates to your goals and the role that you play in society. Things such as being in a new environment, bad experiences, your perceptions of others and knowing the perceptions that others have of you; can cause you to have an identity crisis.

Young people in particular, are struggling with identity crisis. We are living in the social media epidemic, and the majority of our time is spent on it.

There are lots of advantages to using social media. The disadvantages however, are that young people are always comparing themselves to the celebrities and other people that they follow on social media, referring to them as *"Goals"*.

This is a big issue because the more time they spend obsessing over these people on social media, the further they become insecure about themselves.

I can't lie, there have been many times where I've been scrolling through my Instagram feed, or "preeing" as some would say and have ended up in the same boat. I'd be comparing myself to other people, thinking, "I wish I could look as good as her", "These guys are squad goals...I don't even have a squad". "I wish someone could love me like that", "Their lives are so much better than mine". This is the reason why I occasionally take a break from the app.

Having those thoughts can be dangerous because as you focus your attention on the identity of others, your own identity is most likely to become distorted.

Sometimes, the same people who appear to be flawless are simply making good use of filters and makeup; real talk! Also, the ones who are always surrounded by people in photos and look happy, are sometimes sad and lonely in reality. Do not live in comparison; things are not always as they seem.

Having an Identity crisis, could also stem from being uncertain about your career path. Maybe you're currently in a career that's unfulfilling, and you want to leave, but you don't know what career to go into next. Maybe you're unemployed, and you just don't know what to do with your life. Maybe you're self-employed, but things haven't gone according to plan. It happens. Don't beat yourself up about it, have faith and pray for God to guide you in the right direction.

When I was a little girl, I always said that I wanted to be a school teacher when I grew up. Years later, I got a job working as a Teaching Assistant in a primary school. It's there that I decided...I'm not about that life! So dreams can change sometimes.

Identity crisis was my biggest struggle when I was younger. I was extremely shy, so it wasn't always easy for me to fit in. Even though I'm more confident now, fitting in is still a struggle sometimes.

For secondary school, I went to an all-girls school called Highbury Fields. At first, I wasn't feeling it at all; the thought of being stuck with girls for five years of my life made me cringe. It so happened though, that a lot of people in school liked me and I was accepted in all the different squads within the school.

It felt great to be accepted, but the problem was that I would sometimes try to adopt the identity of others; knowing full well that their attitude and lifestyle was without a doubt contrary to my faith. As Christians, we need to be very mindful of the people that we surround ourselves with.

Although I was very quiet in school, I had really crude conversations with people. At the time, I just enjoyed the attention that I received. In spite of all that, I still claimed to be a true Christian, trying to act all holy, when I was far from it. I was living by a double standard. Identity crisis! It didn't take long for me to realise that I was a hypocrite. I ruined my witness, and I regret it.

I understand that putting on a false identity, can be a coping mechanism. A way of coping with peer pressure and adapting to culture and society, but it's not right. As Christians, we are supposed to stand out and as tough as that can be, it's necessary. It's what God expects of us.

Please don't put on a facade in order to fit in, be your authentic self! It's so important to remember that your identity is not just skin deep; your lifestyle and certain decisions that you choose to make will affect your identity.

Identity in Christ

It's pivotal that you know who you are in Christ. The enemy is determined to destroy your identity in Christ. He loves to attack the mind. He knows that if he has your mind, he has you; so he plays mind games.

Have you ever felt insecure? Have you ever been uncertain regarding your identity? Do you doubt your abilities? Do you doubt God? If the answer is yes, then that might be Satan at work!

That's exactly why *Ephesians 6:17* says, *"take the helmet of salvation"*. Put it on and protect your mind! Protect it with the word of God! At one point in my life, I was feeling really low and the devil was attacking my mind.

I decided to write prayers on notecards to fight back and build up my faith. I discovered that the more I read those prayers out loud repeatedly, the stronger my faith became.

Seeing that the method was working for me, I took it a step further and put positive quotes and Bible verses up on my bedroom door (e.g. *"I can do all things through Christ which strengthens me"*, *"For God has not given me the Spirit of fear but of power and of love and of a sound mind."*) I also made a list of all the things that I am in Christ, and I recite them almost every day. It's been life-changing for me!

You can try my method or even something completely different like listening to Gospel music or preachers on YouTube. Find what works for you and NEVER stop encouraging yourself in the Lord.

A child of God who is confident and fully aware of their Identity in Christ, is Satan's worst nightmare. There is so much power in knowing who you truly are. When you know who you are in Christ, you'll find yourself on the road to being who God has called you to be. Satan knows this, which is why he persistently tries to make you lose your identity.

In *Romans 12:2,* the verse begins with *"Be not conformed to this world."* Meaning that you should be set apart. When someone comes in contact with you, they should see that you are different by looking at your lifestyle and the way that you present yourself.

The next part of the verse says *"but be ye transformed by the renewing of your mind".* The devil can't get a firm grip on you when your mind is renewed. You can renew your mind through prayer; ask God to redirect your thoughts, enabling you to think good things and speak positive things over your life.

Remove yourself from distractions, be consistent in studying the word of God. Also, memorise scriptures so that they will remain in your heart and mind. When the enemy comes with his lies, you can rebuke him and remind him of the truth.

PURPOSE

You are NOT who he says you are, but you ARE who God says you are! The devil is a liar, but God is not a man that he should lie. Trust and believe in God's word.

Below are some of the scriptures that encouraged me. You can use them to encourage yourself also.

Psalms 139:14
YOU WERE MADE WONDERFULLY; GOD MAKES NO MISTAKES

I will praise you for I am fearfully and wonderfully made, marvellous are your works and that my soul knoweth right well.

2 Corinthians 5:17
YOU ARE MADE NEW

Therefore, if anyone is in Christ, they are a new creature. Old things have passed away; behold, all things are become new.

Romans 8:37
YOU ARE MORE THAN A CONQUEROR

In all these things we are more than conquerors through him that loved us.

Psalm 103:8
YOU ARE LOVED

The LORD is merciful and gracious, slow to anger and abounding in steadfast love.

Philippians 4:19
YOU ARE BLESSED

My God shall supply all your needs according to his riches in Glory by Christ Jesus.

Deuteronomy 31:6
YOU ARE NEVER ALONE

The Lord your God goes with you; he will never leave you nor forsake you.

KNOW YOUR WORTH!

NOTES

CHAPTER 2

YOUR WORDS HAVE POWER

CHAPTER 2

YOUR WORDS HAVE POWER

Growing up, I would always hear the famous saying, "Sticks and stones may break my bones, but words will never hurt me." I've realised that this statement is not entirely true. Words can hurt! Your words have the power to bring joy, strength, motivation and inspiration but also have the power to discourage, demotivate and destroy.

The word of God contains a range of scriptures about the tongue and how it should be used. *James 3:5* says *"the tongue is a small member, yet it boasts of great things. How great a forest is set ablaze by such a small fire."*

The tongue is used for good and evil. In this verse, it's likened to a fire and just like a fire setting a forest ablaze, your words can burn others spiritually, emotionally and mentally. When words are expressed in a disrespectful and insulting manner, it can ruin relationships.

There are certain people, who have a tendency of wording things in the wrong way because their mouths have no filter. As a result of this, they end up offending people unintentionally.

When someone is offended by you and if it's an ongoing cycle, that person will most likely start avoiding you and may become resentful towards you. This can be avoided by thinking before you speak, so that the right words can come out of your mouth.

PURPOSE

Ephesians 4:29 says *"Do not let any unwholesome talk come out of your mouths, but only what is helpful for building others up according to their needs, that it may benefit those who listen."*

Unwholesome talk includes things such as gossiping, swearing, belittling, hateful comments, arrogant statements, lying, etc. Those things are not pleasing to God. Your words should be edifying and encouraging to whoever is listening to you. Build people up, don't break them down!

The Bible says that *'A gentle answer turns away wrath, but harsh words stir up anger.' – Proverbs 15:1.* It's not every day fight fire with fire; sometimes, fight fire with water!

If someone says something to you out of anger, you responding back in the same way will just cause anger to increase, which will lead to the situation escalating. Your words and the way you use them will either defuse the situation or add fuel to the fire.

I know responding with a gentle answer can be challenging, but it is the right thing to do. It is the wise thing to do. It is God's will that you try your best to live at peace with everyone. Ask God to help and guide you so that when you respond to people, you will answer with gentleness.

In *James 1:19*, the instruction is given: *"My dear brothers and sisters, take note of this: Everyone should be quick to listen, slow to speak and slow to become angry."* It's crucial that you take heed to this scripture. Many relationships have failed due to people not abiding by this verse.

One thing in particular that destroys relationships, is making wrong assumptions. I've been guilty of this. Assuming the worst about some people to the point where I'd become so angry and ignore them, only to find out that it was all just a big misunderstanding on my part.

Ecclesiastes 3:7 reads that there is *"a time to be silent and a time to speak."* I heard someone say, that now and again, we need "The Spirit of Shutup". I definitely agree! Your mouth can get you into trouble, if used in the wrong way and at the wrong time. There are certain situations where you just need to refrain from talking.

If you are one of those people, who feel the need to always have the last word, stop it! Swallow your pride. Your last word may just start a war. Why start a war when you can live peaceably?

Also, you need to be aware that there are certain things that you can't say to everyone. Some individuals are more sensitive than others. What one person might take as a joke, another might find unfunny and hurtful.

In a situation where your words have hurt someone, be sensitive towards that person and apologise to them. A genuine apology goes a long way.

The tongue is sharp like a sword, and once it pierces you, it can leave you with deep wounds that take a long time to heal. *Proverbs 18:21* states that *"death and life are in the power of the tongue: and they that love it shall eat the fruit thereof."*

PURPOSE

That's deep!

This verse of scripture brought my attention to "Word curses". Word curses, are the negative words that have been spoken over you, or that you have spoken over others. When negative words and rude remarks are spoken, it can seriously affect a person's self-confidence and be a huge hindrance to their growth and success.

Oftentimes, the sender is entirely oblivious to the severity of their words. They move on, forgetting they even said anything, while the recipient, lives their life constantly battling the curse.

I can relate to this because I've lived it! There were certain things that were said to me as a young girl that stayed with me years after. Even more recently, negative comments were made about me and I took it to heart. Believing those things caused me to have a poor self-image and body image.

There are many accounts of people who were told that they would never amount to anything when they were young. Even when they reached adulthood, those words ring in their ears, causing them to be burdened with low self-esteem and other issues. Maybe this is something that's happened to you. If it is, I'm sorry that you had to go through that. It's a terrible thing to experience.

In the scripture (*Genesis 35:18*), Rachel is dying due to childbirth. With her last breath, she names her new-born son '*Ben- oni*', which means "the son of my sorrow". Her husband

Jacob, not wanting his son to live with such a depressing and negative name, quickly renames him Benjamin, meaning "son of the right hand".

The right hand represents power, honour, strength and authority! Benjamin had all of these things and grew up to be a great warrior! The Benjamite tribe was named after him and was the smallest out of all the tribes, but all the men in that army were referred to as "Men of valour", as they were all courageous. Thank God Jacob changed the boy's name!

When people constantly speak negatively towards you and you believe what they say, it can have an effect on the way in which you identify yourself. Evidently, what you think is what you will become.

This is why I loved watching videos of DJ Khaled interacting with his son, Asahd. He always speaks love, positivity and blessings over his son's life. Asahd is just a toddler, yet DJ Khaled is already speaking things into existence.

He tells Asahd things like, "You're a legend", "You're an icon", "You're so blessed" and more. When encouraging words like that are instilled in a child at a young age, it's so empowering. That child is most likely to grow up with confidence and a positive attitude towards life. My prayer is that you will implement this approach. Use your words for the blessing and uplifting of others and yourself.

There is an Italian professor by the name of Fabrizio Benedetti.

PURPOSE

He wanted to test the "nocebo effect" and took 100 of his students on a trip into the Italian Alps.

A few days before the actual trip took place, Benedetti shared with one of the students, that the thin air at high altitudes would cause severe migraines.

When it was time to go on the trip now, rumours about the migraine spread to one-quarter of the group. The students that heard the rumour and believed it experienced terrible migraines.

The study proved that negative thoughts could create bad health. The students believed that they would have migraines and they ended up having migraines. In the same way, if you believe that you will fail, then you will fail. If you believe that you can't progress, you won't progress. If you go through life believing that you are defeated, how will you ever conquer?

It all comes down to what you choose to accept. Continuously ask the Lord to transform your mind so that you will be conditioned to accept good things and reject bad things.

Also, *Matthew 12:34-36* reads, *"For out of the abundance of the heart the mouth speaks."* In other words, the words that you speak will reflect the state of your heart.

If your heart is full of anger and hatred, hurtful and hateful words will flow out of your mouth. If your heart is full of love and kindness, words of love and kindness will flow out of your mouth. What is the current state of your heart?

There is a young gospel artist called Jonathan McReynolds,

and he has a song that says "We are Christ representers". Amen! As a Christ representer, your words must be full of grace and your light must shine.

A true Christian is Christ-like — a representation of who Jesus is. The nature of Jesus is Love. So, how can you profess to know and love Jesus but have no love for others and filter for your mouth? Being a Christian is a lifestyle. Self-evaluate. Are you honestly living the life of a Christian or just wearing the title?

__James 1:26__ – If anyone among you thinks he is religious, and does not bridle his tongue but deceives his own heart, this one's religion is useless.

NOTES

CHAPTER 3

THE POWER OF PRAISE & WORSHIP

CHAPTER 3

THE POWER OF PRAISE & WORSHIP

Praise and worship is vital and will often set the tone for the rest of the service. Although there is a correlation between praise and worship; the two words have different meanings.

To praise God is to give Him thanks for what He has done. So, praise is simply an expression of thanksgiving unto God. The Bible says *"Make a joyful noise unto the Lord"* (*Psalm 100*). This can be done through singing, shouting, dancing, clapping, etc. You can also give praise to other people, in appreciation for things they've done or who they are.

Worship, on the other hand, is more intimate than praise, and only God is deserving of worship. In *John 4:24*, Jesus says *"they that worship him, must worship him in spirit and in truth"*.

To worship in spirit means to worship God with your whole heart. Worshipping in truth means to know the God that you worship and have knowledge and understanding of His word (which is the truth). This is the essence of true worship.

Praise is about giving thanks, and worship is about humility and surrender. If you surrender every aspect of your life to God, placing His will above yours, God will be glorified in your life.

Having a heart of surrender, is often an area that young people struggle in. We only want to give God certain parts of our lives as opposed to giving Him everything. We like to be in control and want to do things our way and create our own paths in life, but...there is only one God.

He has orchestrated our lives; so, why are we trying to take over His role? I know that unbelief and doubt are the reasons for lack of surrender to God. Doubting that He will genuinely meet us at the point of our needs. Just know that regardless of your situation, God can bring you through, if it's in His will to do so. So, let your worship rise!

We were created to worship Him. *(Isaiah 43:6).* There are numerous scriptures on the topic of singing praises and worshipping God, which shows how important worship is.

I have to be honest with you; when the Lord gave me this chapter, I was reluctant to include it in this book because I knew that I wasn't a true worshipper. I still need to go deeper in worship.

I rarely dance and lift my hands in church, because I often feel uncomfortable doing those things, especially as I'm positioned right at the front.

There have also been many times in the past, where I've gone to church with the mentality of "I'll clap my hands, but I'm not singing the songs". "I'll only sing and worship God, if the Praise and Worship team sing 'Alpha and Omega'; 'The Anthem', or 'Hosanna' because those are my tunes". This is not the right attitude to have, and it's disrespectful to God.

Looking back, I remember seeing people in church praising and worshipping God, to the point where they fell to the floor and started rolling. In my mind I thought, "Woah. Nahhh...this is not for me mate!"

Now that I'm older, I understand that not everyone will have that experience. Even if that did happen to me, I shouldn't be embarrassed about it. (It's okay, as long as the saints cover me with that white sheet).

Sometimes I still feel conscious of people looking at me and having different perceptions of me in church. So, I often try to keep my composure and quench God's Spirit. This is pride, and the Lord doesn't like it.

Have you ever been deep in praise and worship, and suddenly, from the corner of your eye, you see someone staring at you? You turn to look at them, and realise they weren't staring at you. It is Satan's method of distraction; he'll do anything to prevent you from connecting with Jesus.

In a situation like that, you have to redirect your focus. Close your eyes if you can and keep your mind focused on Christ so that you can block out distractions. Don't allow Satan to steal God's glory. Instead, give God the glory that is due unto His name (Psalm 29:2).

I heard someone say, "Worship gets God's attention and brings you to a new dimension." When God hears and receives your worship, He will respond.

Also, don't leave worshipping to the older saints and the deep saints. Worship is for you too. You can be young and worship God. You can be young and live for God.

If we were created to worship and honor God, but don't do that, then we dishonor Him. Your place in heaven is determined by your ability to honour Him on earth. Worship is a lifestyle.

In saying that, there are many distractions and situations that you may face in life. If you're not careful, those things can become idols. The more you idolise them, is the more they will become the focus of your worship. Whatever you give the most attention to will become your God.

There is so much power in worship, but how can you experience it for yourself if your attention is elsewhere? God inhabits the praises of His people (*Psalms 22:3*), meaning when you praise and worship Him, He will be in the midst. When the praises go up, the blessings come down. Don't you want to receive every blessing that God has for you? I know I do! I desire to have a heart of worship.

A great example of the power of worship is found in *Acts 16* which is about two men called Paul and Silas. They were stripped, humiliated publicly, severely beaten and thrown into prison.

After that terrible ordeal, you'd think they would be angry and try to come up with an escape plan or something. Instead, Paul and Silas prayed and sang praises unto God. They worshipped God in the midst of trouble.

In verse 26, it says *"Suddenly, there was such a violent earthquake, that the foundations of the prison were shaken. At once all the prison doors flew open, and everyone's chains came loose.*

Imagine a worship so powerful that it shakes an entire building and shifts the atmosphere! God recognised that their worship came from a genuine place, so as they sent worship up. In response, God sent an immediate blessing down. The power of God was evident.

The chains that were securely fastened were no match for the power of God. Worship has the power to break the physical and spiritual chains in your life. If you are bound in any way, I'm telling you, the key to your breakthrough is in your worship.

While reading this scripture, I was reminded of Job who lost all his possessions; his children died, and on top of that, he was plagued with a disease that left him with terrible sores all over his body.

Although Job felt very low at times, he still had faith in God. In his darkest hour, he didn't 'curse God and die' like his wife told him to. Instead, he said, "Though he slay me, yet will I trust him." WOW. "Yet will I trust him". That's such a powerful declaration to make.

Job had no idea when his change would come, yet he trusted God. In the end, God restored everything that Job lost. Job was blessed with double the amount that he had before!

I believe Paul and Silas had a similar mentality to Job, declaring, "We've been beaten, humiliated and thrown into prison, yet we will worship!" Worship was their posture, so even through pain and hard trials, worship was the first resort.

What is your posture in the midst of the storm? Like these three men of God, make worship your posture. Did you lose your job? Worship. Did your friends turn away? Worship.
Stop focusing on your problems and focus on Jesus, the way-maker.

One of my main inspirations in the Bible has to be brother David. I love reading about this guy. In *Samuel 6 verse 14*, David was worshipping God for the Ark of the Covenant being in his city.

The verse says *"David danced before the Lord with all his might."* He worshipped God with everything he had—his whole heart!

In verse 20 of that same chapter, David returns home and is greeted by his wife Michal, a.k.a Mrs Naggy. She witnessed him dancing and felt like he was behaving inappropriately for a king. She mentions how David "uncovered himself"; this tells me that he was dancing out of his clothes. Brother David was going in!!

David's first response was, "It was before the Lord". He really didn't care about his royal status or who was looking at him and how people would perceive him. None of that mattered to him; David just wanted to praise and worship his God.

Let us have the spirit of David and worship without holding back, not being so proud and concerned with status and popularity, unashamed! I want to get to that place. I will get to that place in Jesus name! You can get there too. If you're in that place already, praise God! Keep going, continue to have a heart of worship.

I sincerely thank God for this chapter. The same words that you have read are the exact words that God has used to speak to and convict me. My prayer is that this chapter will evoke change and bring out the worshipper in you. Amen.

NOTES

CHAPTER 4

THE ATTRIBUTES OF JESUS

CHAPTER 4

THE ATTRIBUTES OF JESUS

It's essential that you know who Jesus is, so I've written this chapter as a reminder for you. I know you might be tempted to skip this chapter if you feel like you already know Jesus. You may have read about Him in the Bible, studied the scriptures, and pray to Him.

All that is good, but do you remember who He is when your life doesn't go the way you want it to go? Do you remember who He is when people hurt and disappoint you? Do you remember who He is when your prayers are not answered when you want them to be?

You can't afford to forget who Jesus is. Maybe you partially know of Jesus as the one your family members pray to and serve, but don't really know Him for yourself.

If you look at your relationships, whether it be with family, friends or a romantic partner, there is often a level of intimacy that you share with them. This enables you to trust and depend on them. Likewise, the more you know who Jesus is, the further you will put your trust and dependence on Him.

Jesus has amazing attributes, and these attributes can be identified when you read about His life, even till His death on the cross. Also, because Jesus lives, He still demonstrates those attributes today. I've listed some of Jesus' attributes below.

Compassionate

In the Bible, there are so many examples of Jesus showing compassion to others. Jesus travelled all over, preaching, teaching, and healing people because he genuinely loved them and wanted them to be saved. The same Jesus in the Bible, is the same Jesus today. He never gets tired of caring for you.

The word compassion derives from the latin word 'compati' which means "to suffer with". Jesus feels your pain and he knows what you're going through.

Isaiah 30:18 says "Yet the Lord longs to be gracious to you; therefore he will rise up to show you compassion..." Amen. Jesus has great compassion for you.

Loving

Jesus demonstrated His love for mankind when He gave His life on the cross. Jesus had the power to come down from the cross, but He stayed there. It was love that kept Him there.

Also, Jesus listens and answers prayers. In *John 10:14,* Jesus refers to Himself as "The good shepherd". The role of a shepherd is to look after and protect the sheep as a father would do for his child.

There is a song that describes Jesus as being a "Good Good Father". In the song, there is a part that says that Jesus is

THE ATTRIBUTES OF JESUS

perfect in all His ways and consistent in every way. Amen!

Friends and family may stop loving you for whatever reason. Earthly fathers will fail sometimes; some are present but don't know how to love. Others choose to be absent from their child's life, but Jesus is consistent in loving you. If no one else loves you, know that Jesus loves you.

Forgiving

Jesus is certainly forgiving. He was deserted by His disciples, who were supposed to be His friends. He was brutally tortured to the point where He was unrecognisable. He was mocked, spat on and stripped. He was humiliated and publicly shamed!

Yet, through all of that, the words that came out of His mouth were, *"Father forgive them, for they know not what they do." (Luke 24:34)*. Jesus is the greatest example of forgiveness. Even when we make mistakes and go down the wrong paths in life, he's still merciful, he's still forgiving. He still has his arms outstretched for us.

Jesus wants you to follow His example and forgive others. It's not easy, but it's not impossible either. Figuratively speaking, you should never be so quick to throw stones and cut people off. Instead, you should adopt the nature of Jesus and show mercy towards them. *(Romans 3:23 – For all have sinned, and come short of the glory of God.)*

Faithful

Jesus' heart was so heavy in the moments leading up to His death. He was deeply saddened, knowing the pain and suffering that He would have to endure.

Hence, the reason He went to the Garden of Gethsemane and prayed the same prayer thrice. *"My Father, if it is possible, may this cup be taken from me, yet not as I will but as you will."*

In other words, Jesus was asking God if it was possible for Him not to die, or to die differently. I love that He says *"yet not as I will but as you will"*. That's faithfulness right there!

Jesus chose to place God's will above His and remained faithful until the very end. Jesus is still faithful, he's faithful to you and I and His word stands forever. If His word stands forever, it means that He's faithful forever. In *Psalm 89:4*, God says *"I will not break my covenant nor alter what my lips have uttered"*. What an amazing God!

Holy

The definition of 'Holy' is to be set apart and sacred. That is who Jesus is. Jesus is incomparable; He is the epitome of perfection. When the Prophet Isaiah had a vision, he saw Seraphim, praising the Lord saying *"Holy, Holy, Holy is the Lord of hosts." (Isaiah 6:3).* The fact that this attribute of God is repeated thrice affirms how incredibly holy He is.

Thinking about the extent of God's holiness can make you

feel so unworthy and far away from Him. If that's how you feel, I just want you to know that He's not far away from you.

Strong tower

When I think of the words "strong tower", it makes me think of a battle. In a battle, the army with the highest castle wall and stronger defence system in place, are the strongest army.

Jesus is a strong tower because He is mighty and is above everyone and everything. Jesus is your strong tower, so there is no need to be afraid. *(Proverbs 18:10 – The name of the Lord is a strong tower, the righteous run into it and are safe.)*

Deliverer

Jesus is a strong deliverer; In many accounts throughout the Bible, Jesus delivered people from sickness, diseases, blindness, demons, etc. The list goes on. Jesus is still delivering today!

Jesus is a strong deliverer, so you can trust Him to deliver you from whatever it is that you are facing. *(Isaiah 43:2)*

Understanding

Jesus understands; He gets you. He knows what it feels like to be heartbroken. He knows what it feels like to be lonely. He knows what it feels like to be betrayed. He knows what it feels like to be humiliated.

Jesus knows what it feels like to feel pain and be beaten. He knows what it feels like to be scared. He knows what it feels like to lose someone you love. You can bring your problems to Jesus, knowing that He will hear and understand. *(Hebrews 4:15-16).*

Patient

Jesus is very patient with us. When I look at my life, I'm not always strong in my faith. I don't always make Jesus a priority in my life. I don't always feel like going to church, and I don't consistently make the right decisions, but Jesus remains patient with me. He will never stop being patient with you.

I'm so grateful that Jesus is patient because if He weren't, there would be no hope. When I make mistakes, I wouldn't get a chance to repent and change my ways.

Cross-cultural

Jesus liked to mix with people of different cultures and backgrounds. He embraced them; much to the confusion and annoyance of His disciples and others who were around Him.

In *Mark 2:15,* Jesus had a meal with plenty of sinners. Certain people started questioning His actions, and His response was: *"It is not the healthy who need a doctor but the sick. I have not come to call the righteous but sinners to repentance."* Amen.

This is the attitude and approach we should have as young people. Make a difference in your society, reach out to people and tell them about Jesus!

NOTES

CHAPTER 5

HELP! TEMPTATION IS MAD STRONG!

CHAPTER 5

HELP! TEMPTATION IS MAD STRONG!

Young people are experiencing temptation more than ever before. Temptation is no joke; it's literally everywhere now. I just want to make it clear to you though, just in case you didn't know, to be tempted is not a sin. We all experience temptation, but the sin is giving in to temptation.

Mark 14:38 says, *"Watch and pray, so that you will not fall into temptation. The spirit is willing but the flesh is weak."* In your spirit, you might know deep down what the right thing to do is and be willing to do it, but your flesh (ungodly nature and mindset) is weak and can get the better of you.

That's why the verse starts off with "Watch and pray", it's not easy to fight the flesh. For this reason, you must be alert and prayerful always, praying against the works of the flesh.

There are a few people in the Bible who fell into temptation. One of them was King David. In *2ⁿᵈ Samuel 11*, King David stayed back from battle one day, walked on the roof of his palace and witnessed a woman bathing. David liked what he saw, mmmhmm...

The woman's name was Bathsheba (probably because she spent most of her time in the bath, I don't know.) So, to summarize, he sleeps with her, she gets pregnant, and David sets up her husband (Uriah) to be killed. David then marries Bathsheba. The whole situation was a hot mess!

The saying is true "An idle mind is the Devil's playground."

God was displeased with David because David had sinned against Him. So, God punished Him by promising to give all of David's wives to his neighbour and to make it a public display. Also, the Lord allowed David's son to die.

This was painful for both David and Bathsheba. Although David did repent after and was forgiven, all of that pain could've been avoided if David had more self-control and didn't fall into temptation. *James 1:14* says, *"Every man is tempted when he is drawn away by his own lust and enticed."*

Another example is Samson. He was the world's strongest man, and the chosen one to save Israel. Unfortunately, Samson fell in love with a Philistine woman called Delilah. She lured him into revealing the source of his strength to her and then she betrayed him; relaying his secret to the Philistine rulers. What happened to Samson? He lost his strength and was held captive (*Judges 16*).

Samson prayed for God to restore his strength, so that he could kill all the Philistines and die with them. Although God did restore Samson's strength, and he ended up killing more people in his death, than those he killed in his life, he could have accomplished greater things. His story could have ended in a different way.

On a personal note, I have a lot of experience with temptation.

There have been times when I've resisted temptation and times when I've failed to resist temptation.

I've been tempted to cuss people out. BUT GOD!

I've been tempted to be in a relationship with guys that didn't even share my beliefs and standards.

I said that I would keep it 100. Initially, I wasn't going to share this next part, out of fear of being judged and criticised, but I believe it's necessary that I share it. I struggled with an issue for years, an issue that is not often addressed in church. When it is addressed, it's not dealt with in depth.

I feel like there are other young people like myself, who have struggled or are currently struggling with this same issue in silence. So, I'm breaking my silence.

I'm referring to my struggle with pornography. It was introduced to me in my early teens, a moment I wish I could erase. After seeing one video, I just wanted to see more and more. I was addicted to it.

I would feel so guilty for watching it and would ask for God's forgiveness, promising not to watch it again. However, I kept falling into temptation. It was a constant cycle.

I know people in the world may not think it's that deep, but I believe that it is. Young people are taught that it's not a big deal if you watch porn, and that it's okay to pleasure yourself. I disagree. There are probably even some Christians who will argue that there's nothing wrong with doing those things, because you're not actually having sex and there are no scriptures that directly say anything against it.

Yes, that is true. However, the word "lust" is mentioned a number of times in the Bible. Here's what the Bible says about lust. *Matthew 5:28 – "But I tell you that anyone who looks at a woman lustfully has already committed adultery with her in his heart."* Amen. Females are not exempted from this; the same things apply to them if they look at a man lustfully.

In *1st Peter 2:11*, it says *"abstain from fleshly lusts which wage war against the soul."* If you lose your soul, you'll lose the hope of eternal life. Do everything you can to stay away from lust.
The scripture *1st John 2:16* says, *"For everything in the world, the lust of the flesh, the lust of the eyes and the pride of life, comes not from the Father but from the world."*
Lust does not come from God; it emanates from Satan. This means that if you are going against God's will and pleasing the devil, it's not something that should be taken lightly.

How do you overcome temptation? I'm so glad you asked.
In order for you to overcome temptation, you have to truly believe that you are an overcomer. Seek the Lord, pray, fast and have self-control.

The word of God tells us to *"Rejoice in hope; be patient in tribulation and continue instant in prayer" (Romans 12:12)*. Another verse says *"pray without ceasing"*. I always prayed about my struggle, believing God for my deliverance. I also searched on YouTube for videos of people who went through the same thing as me and overcame. Testimonies are encouraging.

I had to separate from things that I knew would cause me to fall back into temptation. For me, that meant separating from my phone when I felt some time of way, not listening to some songs and not watching certain movies, or engaging in certain conversations. Also, you might benefit from having an accountability partner. Someone you can trust, who will support you on your journey towards overcoming.

Those things worked for me, and I thank God because I've been delivered from the addiction! I want to encourage and let you know that if I can conquer temptation, you can too!

1st Corinthians 10:13 says that *"when you are tempted, God will also provide a way out, so that you can endure it"*. Know that there is a way out; you are not a hopeless case!

However, you won't be able to overcome temptation if you continue to feed it. If you surround yourself with drug dealers, you might be tempted to be a drug dealer. You will feed the temptation if you continue to hang around those people.

If you are tempted to "get busy" with that peng girl or peng boy, you will feed the temptation by sliding into the DMs, calling or texting them late at night, answering their late night phone calls and being alone with them. If you're having a conversation and you feel it going in the wrong direction, change the subject.

Starve the temptation! *Galatians 5:16* says, *"Walk in the Spirit and you will not fulfill the lust of the flesh."* The best example of someone who refused to succumb to temptation was Jesus. Jesus had just finished His 40 days fasting and was really hungry. The devil used that as the perfect opportunity to tempt Him.

The devil tried to challenge Jesus to turn stone into bread. Jesus' response was, *"It is written, man shall not live by bread alone."* Satan also tempted Him with kingdoms and authority and attempted to get Jesus to worship him. Jesus' answer to that was, *"It is written: 'Worship the Lord your God and serve him only.'"*

Satan challenged Jesus to throw Himself off the highest point of a temple while quoting *Psalm 91:11-12,* which mentions how God shall give His angels charge over His people and protect them. The devil knows the scriptures! That's even more reason for you to read and study the word of God. It will help you to counteract Satan.

Notice that for every challenge that Satan threw at Jesus, Jesus used God's word as a rebuttal against him. The devil realised that Jesus was not going to fall for temptation, so he stopped tempting him and left. When you are being tempted, the word of God is your spiritual weapon. USE IT!

James 4:7 says, *"Submit yourselves to God, resist the devil and he will flee."* He WILL flee! Amen. So yes, temptation is mad strong, but with Jesus, you'll have the strength to endure and overcome it.

NOTES

CHAPTER 6

WHERE IS MY BOAZ?
WHERE IS MY RUTH?

CHAPTER 6

WHERE IS MY BOAZ? WHERE IS MY RUTH?

"Where is my Boaz?" A question that Christian women often ask the Lord and themselves. I've asked this question many times myself. I know that there are probably some guys asking the question, "Where is my Ruth?"

In the Book of Ruth, you'll see that both Boaz and Ruth had great qualities and attributes. Boaz was God-fearing, respectful, hospitable, understanding, a leader, protector, provider and more. Ruth was a woman who had integrity, she was open-minded, faithful, hardworking, reliable, caring, self-less, obedient and more. These are the kind of attributes that we should desire to have and also look for, and pray for in a spouse.

Prayer is imperative and as mentioned before, there is power in prayer. In singleness, pray for your future spouse. If you're reading this and you're married pray for your spouse and your marriage.

I'm constantly praying for my future husband because I believe in speaking things into existence. I also trust God and believe His word which says that He will give me the desires of my heart *(Psalm 37:4)*. I desire to be married one day and by faith, I believe that it will happen.

I always pray for God to meet my husband at the point of his needs. I pray for his protection and well-being. I pray that he will live a purposeful life. I pray that he will be a man of integrity and like David; he will be a man after God's heart. I pray that he will be a leader, a loving husband and a great father, etc. Speak things into existence!

In praying for your spouse, don't forget to pray for yourself also. Pray that the Lord will work on you and reveal any traits in you that need to be changed or removed. Pray for the willingness to be open to change if needs be.

Also, when you enter into a relationship, you enter into a partnership. In order for the relationship to flourish, there needs to be good communication and team work. "Teamwork makes the dream work." You should pray and ask yourself the question, "What do I bring to the table?" It's important that you add value to your relationship.

One of the things that I think prevents people from finding the love that God has for them, or slows the process down, is "The list" - A list of requirements and expectations of a spouse. Initially, I was going to tell you to scrap the list, but then I realised, having a list is not necessarily a bad thing. (Some people may have been blessed with someone who matched their list.)

It's more about the type of things that you put on the list. In general, the lists that some people have can be very superficial. When I was younger, I had a long list. It consisted of things like "I want a man that can sing" and "I want a tall man" etc.

There are people who only want to be with someone who has a certain job, a specific hair colour, or someone who knows how to drive.

If God brings the husband or wife to them, they may push them away just because the person doesn't tick the boxes on their list. What you want is not always what you need. God knows what you need.

I envisioned that my future husband would be a new member of my church. He would visit and end up falling in love with my church and me. That would be ideal because if we were from two different churches, we'd have to decide on which church to attend together. It's not easy leaving the church that you're comfortable in. I don't think that it would feel right, to be married and going to separate churches. *Mark 10:18* says *"the two will become one flesh"*.

Also, I wanted the same experience that my parents had with love. Their love story is amazing to me. They were in two different parts of the world. My mum was living in London, and my dad was living in Jamaica. God revealed to my dad in a vision, that his future wife was in London and showed him exactly what she looked like.

My dad was blessed with the opportunity to travel to the UK and it so happened that he saw the woman who was in the vision...My mum! He visited his auntie's church, not knowing that my mum was a part of that ministry. God is amazing!

PURPOSE

I heard that my dad enquired about my mum. He spoke to people who knew her in church, to find out more about her and what they thought of her. Everyone gave him positive feedback. Take notes! It can be really beneficial to enquire about someone that you might be interested in. The people closest to them, will know more about them than you do. So to cut a long story short, my parents got married and a year later, they had a bundle of joy called Lydia.

That was their story, but the truth of the matter is, not everyone will have the same story. Maybe you'll meet the love of your life in church and maybe you won't. My advice to you, is to be open-minded about love.

Maybe you planned to be married at a certain age, and that age has come and gone, and you're still single. Perhaps things didn't work out, with that person that you thought you would spend the rest of your life with.

Maybe you've been fantasising about how you will fall in love and your whole marriage process. However, things may not happen in the way you intend for them to occur. God says *"my thoughts are not your thoughts, neither are your ways my ways"*.

Another piece of advice that I'll give you is: *don't settle for someone, just to fill a void*. Sometimes, the desire to be in a relationship can be so strong, that you might just feel like settling for some next man or some next woman. Having the mentality of "I can change them".

Being with the wrong person can cause you a great deal of pain, heartache, stress and frustration. Why? Because they are not for YOU! Yes, people can change, but is it worth putting your heart on the line, in the hope that it will happen?

Proverbs 4:23 says, *Guard your heart above all else, for it determines the course of your life.*

If you're in a relationship with someone that you know you're not supposed to be with, and God has warned you to break it off, break it off! Lock it off! Let it go! It won't work, if it's not meant to be. I understand that it can be hard to let go of someone that you have strong feelings for, but holding on to them might be bad for you in the long run.

In addition, you shouldn't enter into a relationship with someone, if your heart is with another person. When you get married, it will be difficult to give your all in the marriage because your whole heart is not in it. Marriage is a big deal and a big step. It's so important to get closure before embarking on the journey. It's also important to take your time and make sure that you're with someone for the right reasons.

Also, I strongly believe that a person who is genuinely interested in you, will make time for you. If they were truly interested in you, then you would cross their mind, and they would keep in touch with you. If there is no effort made on their part, don't bend over backwards to try and make them love you...let it go darling.

Now, if it's a situation where you are certain that the Lord has confirmed who you will marry, but the person has not shown any interest in you, it's likely to be the right person at the wrong time. If you go up to the person and say "God says you are my spouse, we must be together now!" You might push them even further away. Please don't do that.

God may have given you a revelation about your future, rather than your present. Just wait on the Lord and continue to serve him, if it's in God's will, when the time is right, I believe that he will bring you and the other person together. Don't rush love. If you rush love, you could block or delay meeting the right person for you. I'm sure you don't want that.

Proverbs 16:9 says *"In their hearts, humans plan their course, but the Lord establishes their steps".* Allow the Lord to establish your steps. You may have certain family members and friends, who are constantly putting pressure on you to get married. Don't let them get to you, bring up that scripture and remind them that God is in control.

I know that for many young Christian women like myself, the frustrating thing is, there's a lack of Christian men in the church. In fact, in my whole life, I think I've only seen one church that has lots of men, and I've been to a number of churches.

I asked one of my male friends, for his thoughts on the issue of there being a lack of men in the church, as I wanted to get a male perspective. His response was that pride is a big issue. Men don't want to surrender or submit to God because they don't want to be vulnerable, and believe they can handle things on their own.

He also mentioned that the devil is tempting men with worldly desires, and they feel like they don't need God. I also think that maybe, some men may be intimidated by the number of women in the church. These things make it hard for them to come in or be committed.

I asked another male Christian friend, if he was attracted to any of the young women in his church. He said that they were like his sisters and he didn't see them on a romantic level. I found that interesting, and that's probably how some other Christian men feel too.

For others, maybe they feel attracted to a church sister but have a fear of being rejected or other church members getting involved. In some churches, there are more married couples than singles. This makes the prospect of finding love in church slim. I believe that these are some of the reasons for the amount of single people in churches.

Christian women are taught to wait on God and to wait for men to find them; as men are supposed to be the pursuers. Two scriptures that are often used to back this up are *Proverbs 18:22* – *"He who finds a wife finds a good thing"*, and *Proverbs 31:10*, which says *"who can find a virtuous woman? For her price is far above rubies"*.

PURPOSE

If you are someone who rarely goes out, you just hide away at home waiting for God to drop "The one" from the sky. I encourage you to change your routine and your way of thinking. Go out and socialize with others when you can. That's how you meet people and build relationships. Your future partner might be at an event or social gathering; you never know.

Another point that I'd like to make, is on making your interests known to a person. Boaz and Ruth both made their interests known to one another. Boaz showed that he was interested in Ruth through his actions; he protected her and provided for her.

Ruth really showed her true interest in Boaz, by lying at his feet on the threshing floor and telling him to spread his garment over her, as he was the guardian-redeemer of her family *(Ruth 3:9)*. Boaz then proceeded to make Ruth his wife.

If you're interested in someone, it's okay to show it. Smile with them, don't be dismissive but be approachable and friendly towards them and let them know how you feel.

Christian men are taught to wait on God. The problem is, some Christian women are waiting for Christian men to pursue them, but they are not being pursued.

Frustration and impatience, sometimes leads to Christians choosing to be in relationships with unbelievers. The scripture clearly tells us, *"Do not be unequally yoked with unbelievers"* – *2nd Corinthians 6:14.* That's the part of the verse that gets the most attention, but the rest of the verse goes on to say,

"For what do righteousness and wickedness have in common? Or what fellowship can light have with darkness?" Amen.

If a Christian and an unbeliever are in a relationship, of course, they will be unequally yoked, as they'll have different beliefs. Also, I think that when there are children involved, it can be difficult to raise them in the right way. It can cause so much conflict and drama. I'm not about that life at all. It's God's will for us to be in Godly relationships.

I went to a seminar for single Christian women once, and the speaker mentioned that she was thinking about having a social event, where single Christians can come together and mingle with each other. I believe that it's a great idea. Some young people don't know any Christians from other churches. An event like this will help more young Christians to connect with each other. I think that great success could come out of it.

Also, it's important to seek counsel from your church leaders or God-fearing family members; if you have an interest in someone and feel like you're ready for marriage. Even if you haven't met anyone, it will help to discuss marriage with those who are more experienced in that area. They'll be able to give you Godly direction and advice and will also pray with you and for you.

In the past, I prayed to God concerning certain guys that were interested in me and who I was also interested in. This didn't happen in one moment, but at different time periods of my life. I asked the Lord continuously, to reveal if they were right for me. God literally answered my prayers through a number of dreams; revealing that those guys were not for me. It was clear as day! I made the decision to distance myself from them and I know it was the right decision.

God listens and God speaks. He speaks in various ways. Seek God about your significant other, and make yourself available to hear from Him.

In *Ruth 3: 11*, look at what Boaz says to Ruth, "All the people of my town know that you are a woman of noble character." Ruth's character spoke volumes and made her stand out. She was recognized by many people, as being a virtuous woman. Also, her character is what Boaz was mostly attracted to. So, having a good character is crucial and you should want to be with someone who has a good character.

Furthermore, don't just accept someone because they claim to believe in Jesus. Many people claim to believe in Jesus, but don't really walk with him. Observe their character. How do they carry themselves? How do they deal with people? How do they handle certain situations? Be mindful of these things.

There are many scriptures relating to husbands and wives in the Bible. For example, *Ephesians 5: 22-23 which says, "Wives, submit yourselves to your own husbands as you do to the Lord. For the husband is the head of the wife as Christ is the head of the church..."*

Studying scriptures relating to this topic is great, because they highlight the qualities and actions of a godly man and woman. Through studying these scriptures, singles and young married couples, can develop a better understanding of what is required of them in a marriage and also how to sustain the marriage.

Although there is nothing wrong with having a desire to be married, you shouldn't allow the thought of marriage to consume your mind. Make the most of singleness when you're in it. Achieve your goals and do things that you love.

Singleness is a growing period, don't abuse it. In singleness, work on yourself and develop your character. Work on your communication skills; especially if communicating is something that you struggle with. Lack of communication in a relationship, is like a ship without a sail. Disastrous!

Work on being patient with others. Maybe even travel more; see the world. Work on submission. Learn how to budget and save money, learn how to cook if you don't know how to. Learn to love and embrace yourself in singleness. If you don't love yourself, you'll make it hard for someone to love you. I imagine that working on yourself in singleness, will also help you to have an easier transition into marriage.

Most importantly, always put God first. Boaz and Ruth exist and might be closer than you think they are. Don't rush love and start moving reckless. Be patient, remain dignified and trust that your Heavenly Father will come through for you.

NOTES

CHAPTER 7

THE FRUIT OF THE SPIRIT

CHAPTER 7

THE FRUIT OF THE SPIRIT

It was so vital for me to include this chapter. The fruit of the Spirit is something that is essential for Christians to have, yet it is not always taken seriously and often overlooked.

Some people proudly call themselves 'Christians' but don't bear the fruit of the Spirit. I admit that I have been guilty of this plenty of times. The fact of the matter is that a true Christian is identified by the fruit that they bear.

The fruit of the Spirit is mentioned in the Book of *Galatians 5.* In verse 17 of that same chapter, it explains that the Spirit is at war with the flesh. The Spirit, being the Holy Spirit, helps you to live right, and the flesh, being your sinful nature, causes you to do wrong.

From verses 19–21, the Bible explains what the works of the flesh are. It reads, *"Now the works of the flesh are manifest, which are these; adultery, fornication, uncleanness, lasciviousness, idolatry, witchcraft, hatred, variance, emulations, wrath, strife, seditions, heresies, envyings, murders, drunkenness, revellings, and such like...they which do such things shall not inherit the kingdom of God."*

I don't know about you, but for the longest time, I would read that passage, knowing that the works of the flesh were bad, but not having a full understanding of what some of those words meant.

The Bible says that if you do those things, you shall not inherit the kingdom of God. It's that serious! It's essential that you know what they mean. So, I've put the words and the meanings below.

Adultery	Sexual relations between a married person and someone they are not married to.
Fornication	Sex before marriage.
Uncleanness	Impure morals, lifestyles, thoughts and motives.
Lasciviousness	Lustfulness
Idolatry	Worshipping idols.
Witchcraft	The practice of magic and casting spells. Word curses are also a form of witchcraft; it involves speaking negative things over people's life.
Variance	The act of being inconsistent, argumentative, bitter, spiteful and unfriendly, etc.
Emulations	Jealousy and rivalry
Wrath	Extreme anger
Strife	Bitterness and conflicts
Seditions.	Rebellion
Heresies	Deviation from established beliefs
Revellings	Reckless behaviour and partying wildly.

If you are guilty of any of the above, the Bible does say in *1st John 1:9 – "If we confess our sins, he is faithful and just and*

will forgive us our sins and purify us from all unrighteousness."
However, if you are unrepentant, you will not inherit the kingdom
of God. So, I urge you to repent of your sins wholeheartedly.

Unfortunately, due to the fall of Adam in the Garden of Eden,
mankind inherited the fallen Adamic nature and are inclined to
sin. Although this is true, please don't use the "I'm only human,
God forgives" card as an excuse to remain in sin. Yes, God is
forgiving, but do not abuse His Grace.

Now, *Galatians 5:22* reads: *"But the fruit of the Spirit is love,
joy, peace, longsuffering, gentleness, goodness, faith, meekness,
temperance against such there is no law."* I'm going to elaborate
more on each fruit with supporting scriptures.

LOVE

1st Corinthians 13:13 - *Faith, hope and love, these three. But the
greatest of these is love. (NIV)*

Luke 6:35 - *Love your enemies, do good to them and lend to them
without expecting anything back. Then your reward will be
great...(NIV)*

1st Corinthians 13: 4-8 - *Love is patient, love is kind. It does not
envy it does not boast, it is not proud. (NIV)*

Love is the greatest gift of all because love is eternal and
supreme. Love surpasses all other virtues. In *1st John 4:8*, it says
that *"God is love"*. Loving is who He is. Loving is what He does;

PURPOSE

Love is His nature!

A Christian should be like Christ and emulate Him. Remember that for the people who don't know Jesus, you may be the only Jesus that they see! Don't ruin your witness. Jesus commands you to love your enemies and do good to them without expecting anything in return. He added that your reward would be great if you do!

If you're reading this and thinking, "No way, you must be joking!" NO. I am very serious my friend. If you want to follow Christ, it's crucial that you follow His example.

Jesus died on the cross in such a horrific and painful way, all because He loved you and I. It was love that kept Him on that cross. He gave His life for His friends, as well as His enemies.

I encourage you to follow Christ's example, by showing love to others. If it is difficult for you to be near certain people, love them from a distance and pray for them, but don't refuse to love at all.

Also, another way of showing love is to speak well of people. There is a verse in the Bible which warns that corrupt conversations should not proceed out of the mouth.

So, if you like to cuss people out, it's time to change! If you are a gossiper, it's time to change! I know the gossiping spirit can be mighty strong, but it is unkind to speak negative things about people or over their lives. Gossiping is not a Godly character and it is displeasing to God.

Love is patient; everyone will not have the same mentality

or be at the same level of maturity. Some may be slower than others in specific areas. Don't nurture impatience and look down on people because they are different from you. Instead of knocking people down, build them up and encourage them.

Furthermore, you shouldn't be envious of other people and what they have. Be happy for them and be content with who you are and what you've been blessed with. *"Love does not boast, it is not proud"*, so love is about being humble. The Bible says "God resists the proud but gives Grace to the humble".

Love is also about supporting and comforting those who are going through hard times. You shouldn't be so wrapped up in your own life that you are unaware of what others are going through. Love is selfless.

JOY

James 1: 2 -3 - Consider it pure joy, my brothers and sisters, whenever you face trials of many kinds, because you know that the testing of your faith produces perseverance. (NIV)
1st Thessalonians 5:16–18 - Rejoice evermore. Pray without ceasing. In everything give thanks: for this is the will of God in Christ Jesus concerning you. (KJV)
Romans 12:12 - Rejoicing in hope; patient in tribulation; continuing instant in prayer; (KJV)

It's not always easy to have joy during trials. Believe me, I know! I've experienced being rejected by people and many employers. I've experienced the pain of losing loved ones. The biggest loss for me was losing my Grandma.

When I heard that she passed away, I was so broken and extremely angry because I was crying out to God day and night, begging him to heal my Grandma and allow her to live. I believed that it would happen but it didn't.

For a while I lost faith in God. The joy came, from knowing that my Grandma is in a better place, her legacy lives on and she will forever live on in my heart and in my memories.

If you're going through trials, don't give up! Trials are a test of faith, and with faith comes perseverance. I want you to know that God has NOT forgotten you! He is bigger than your situation. So, choose to have joy regardless of your situation.

PEACE

Hebrews 12:14 - Make every effort to live in peace with everyone and to be holy; without holiness no one will see the Lord. (NIV)

Proverbs 16:7 - When the LORD takes pleasure in anyone's way, he causes their enemies to make peace with them. (NIV)

Isaiah 26:3 - You will keep in perfect peace those whose minds are steadfast, because they trust in you. (NIV)

A Christian should be a peacemaker and do everything that they can to live at peace with others. Peace is holiness, and without holiness, no one can see God.

Communication is a crucial factor of peace; I'll give you an example. There was a time when I felt very disrespected by someone. This person would see me but walk past me like I was invisible. I'd be talking to them, and they wouldn't even give me eye contact.

I don't like confrontation, but I decided to confront the person. I took them to one side and explained to them how I felt very disrespected and annoyed by their behaviour towards me. They apologised to me, and promised to be more alert and respectful from that point onwards.

Since we talked, that person has kept their word, and I'm cool with them now. We're not the best of friends, but we are civil towards one another. That experience showed me the importance of good communication. By being bold enough to confront that person, I was able to make peace and also get my peace of mind.

LONGSUFFERING

Galatians 6:9 - *And let us not grow weary while doing good, for in due season we shall reap if we do not lose heart. (NKJV)*

James 1:3 - *Knowing this, that the trying of your faith worketh patience (KJV).*

Colossians 3:13 - *Bear with each other and forgive one another if any of you has a grievance against someone. Forgive as the Lord forgave you. (NIV)*

PURPOSE

Longsuffering means to have or show patience in troublesome times. Life will not always be a bed of roses; trials will come to test your faith, but you must endure and believe that God will bring you through. HE WILL! Don't worry about the duration of problems, but instead, focus on Jesus who has the power to deliver you.

Also, you shouldn't grow tired of doing good deeds and displaying the fruit of the Spirit. I know it can be very disheartening when your good works are not acknowledged or appreciated.

If you remain persistent in doing good, it's a promise that you will reap the rewards in due season. Your labour will not be in vain. Doing good should be less about pleasing people and more about honouring God.

Longsuffering also means to bear with others and forgive them. If you are incapable of doing this, it will destroy your relationships and offend God as well. It's important to pray for self-control and wisdom in regards to the appropriate way of dealing with people and specific situations.

In *Romans 3:23,* it says: *"For all have sinned and come short of the glory of God."* Despite this, the Lord remains faithful and forgiving and still finds favour in you and I. It is not in His nature to be unforgiving and to not have a longsuffering attitude towards His people.

I'm grateful that the Lord has a heart of forgiveness and

chooses not to turn His back on me when I fail Him. Where would I be without Him? If you don't learn how to forgive others, the Lord will not forgive you when you sin against Him *(Matthew 6:14-15)*. For you to be in right standing with the Lord, it's vital that you mirror His example.

When you demonstrate longsuffering, it doesn't only have a positive effect on you, but it will also have a positive impact on those around you.

GENTLENESS

Proverbs 15:1 - *A gentle answer turns away wrath, but a harsh word stirs up anger. (NIV)*

Colossians 3:12 - *Therefore, as God's chosen people, holy and dearly loved, clothe yourselves with compassion, kindness, humility, gentleness and patience. (NIV)*

Gentleness means to have a humble attitude and a calm approach. There are some people who just don't care about the feelings of others and hurt them intentionally. Then there are others who simply word things in the wrong way and end up offending people by mistake.

Be very careful with the words that proceed from your mouth. Don't speak rashly; think before you speak. If you need to approach someone, you should do so in a gentle manner, and if someone approaches you about something, you should respond with a gentle answer. The Bible says that 'harsh words stir up anger'. When people are angry, situations are likely to escalate and be blown way out of proportion. When gentleness is used, all of that can be avoided.

If you have an argument and you end up saying some awful things out of anger, be quick to apologise and make peace with people. Let go of that spirit of pride! Showing gentleness towards others will also allow you to be a better witness and draw people closer to Jesus.

Self-evaluate. Ask yourself questions like: Did I handle that situation with gentleness? And if not, what could I have done better? Am I living by the example of Jesus Christ?

This will enable you to identify any improvements made, as well as areas that you need to work on. Pray that God will help you to show gentleness instead of retaliating with harsh words and actions.

GOODNESS

Romans 12:21 - Do not be overcome by evil, but overcome evil with good. (NIV)

Galatians 6:10 - Therefore, as we have opportunity, let us do good to all people, especially to those who belong to the family of believers. (NIV).

Ephesians 4:29- Let no corrupt word proceed out of your mouth, but what is good for necessary edification, that it may impart grace to the hearers. (NKJV)

Throughout your life, people may upset you and do evil things to you. When this happens, you shouldn't have your heart set on revenge. That is not how a child of God should react. Instead of stooping to their level, rise above it and overcome evil with good. You can do this by choosing to show kindness to them.

In my previous job, I used to sit at a Reception desk, and I remember when I was fairly new, I would say *hello* to people as they walked through the doors, and a few of my work colleagues would just walk on by, without even looking at me or giving a response.

I decided that I would continue being polite and friendly to my work colleagues that were rude to me. I smiled anytime I saw them and greeted them. Over time, my work colleagues started to treat me better; *"A positive mind brings positive results."* It's amazing how people and situations can change, when you choose to overcome evil with good.

Also, you shouldn't just do good to people who you like and are familiar with such as friends and family. *Galatians 6:10* says that you should do good to ALL people. This includes strangers, people of different faiths and cultures and even your enemies.

The verse also says to do good "especially to those who belong to the family of believers". This is talking about the body of Christ—the church. Believers should be in one accord, loving and caring for one another and encouraging one another. Don't neglect the church brethren

FAITH

2nd Corinthians 5:7 - *For we walk by faith, not by sight. (NKJV)*

James 1:6 - *But when you ask, you must believe and not doubt, because the one who doubts is like a wave of the sea, blown and tossed by the wind. (NIV)*

Romans 10:17 - *So then faith cometh by hearing, and hearing by the word of God. (KJV)*

Followers of Christ exercise faith. What is faith? Well, *Hebrews 11:1* reads: *"Faith is the substance of things hoped for, the evidence of things not seen."* A child of God believes in what they can't see. When they pray, they believe by faith that God will answer their prayers.

Faith stems from hearing the word of God being preached and believing it in your heart to be true. People who are unsaved, struggle with the notion of faith because they have the mentality of "I have to see it to believe it".

They don't believe in God because they can't see or feel Him. What a Christian will call a blessing and a miracle, an unbeliever will call luck and a coincidence.

There's a movie that I really love called *The Preacher's Wife*, and at the end of the movie, a little boy says, "You can't see air, but it doesn't stop you from breathing. You can't see God; it shouldn't stop you from believing." He better preach! Amen!

God's word is the most powerful medicine; it uplifts, it

heals, it restores, it strengthens and more. When I'm weak, the Lord says, *"My strength is made perfect in weakness" (2nd Corinthians 12:9)*. When I'm fearful, I can say, *"For God has not given me the spirit of fear but of power and of love and of a sound mind." (2nd Timothy 1:7)*

When I am sick, my Heavenly Father declares *"I will restore you to health and heal your wounds" (Jeremiah 30:17)*. When I'm in need, *"My God will supply all my needs" (Philippians 4:19)*. When I feel lonely, I say *"He will never leave me nor forsake me" (Deuteronomy 31:6)*.

I have strong faith and will forever stand on the promises of God; He's done incredible things in my life. I encourage you to seek God and study His word more; this is how faith rises.

MEEKNESS

Philippians 2:3 - *Do nothing out of selfish ambition or vain conceit. Rather, in humility value others above yourselves. (NIV)*

Proverbs 11:2 - *When pride comes, then comes disgrace, but with humility comes wisdom. (NIV)*

2 Chronicles 7:14 - *If my people, who are called by my name, will humble themselves and pray and seek my face and turn from their wicked ways, then I will hear from heaven, and I will forgive their sin and will heal their land. (NIV)*

The first scripture above states that you should not live your life doing things for selfish ambition or vainglory. In other words, you shouldn't intend to elevate yourself alone and deliberately prevent people from being elevated also.

Never think that you're above others and are more important than them. Humble yourself! Prideful people will make a fool of themselves and bring shame, but humble people have wisdom.

When you are humble, it will also be easier for you to take advice and correction. The Bible says that people will fall without guidance. So, evidently, having wise counsel is needed.

Bearing the fruit of meekness will help you to model Jesus' character and live righteously. The people who are called by God's name are Christians, chosen by God to serve Him and spread the Gospel. We have Jesus within and obtain power from Him.

That's why the Lord says that if we show humility, pray, seek His face and have a heart of repentance, then He will forgive our sins and heal our land. Amen! Our Heavenly Father has given specific guidelines on what needs to be done for our world to be healed.

Sadly, not all Christians find it easy to follow them. We struggle because of lukewarmness. This is not an opinion; it's a fact. Sometimes we pray, yet we lack humility.

Sometimes, we become comfortable in the sins that we commit, and don't repent because we hear about God's grace and mercy. Sometimes, we become so preoccupied with the things of this world that we don't have time to seek the face of God.

I don't know about you, but I want God to heal the world. I need Him to shift the atmosphere. I need Him to open doors; I need Him to break chains and perform miracles! I'm speaking to you and I'm talking to myself when I say, GET IT TOGETHER!

TEMPERANCE

Titus 2:12 - *It teaches us to say "No" to ungodliness and worldly passions, and to live self-controlled, upright and godly lives in this present age. (NIV)*

Proverbs 25:28 - *Like a city whose walls are broken through is a person who lacks self-control. (NIV)*

Temperance is another word for self-control. The Gospel teaches that we should acquire self-restraint, reject worldly pleasures and live righteously.

The Bible says, *"If any man be in Christ, he is a new creature: old things are passed away, behold all things are become new."* When the old nature passes away, it's replaced with a new nature. There should be a transformation, a new love for the things of God and a strong determination to say no to ungodliness. You will still sin at times, as the only perfect one is God Himself, but you will no longer be a slave to sin.

In this world that is full of darkness, the Lord truly wants you to be the light. *"Let your light so shine before men, that they may see your good works, and glorify your Father which is in heaven".*

– *Matthew 5:16.* Amen!

When you lack temperance, your mouth and actions will get you into trouble. You will end up saying the wrong things and expose others as well as yourself. This will put you in danger, and cause you to become vulnerable like a city without walls, and you will gain more enemies than friends. Having temperance is vital.

All the fruit of the Spirit are necessary and profoundly valuable. As young people we need to do our very best to live by them. I pray that you receive a deeper understanding and determination to live by the fruit of the Spirit. The fruit of the Spirit is the nature of Jesus Christ. He longs for you to share His nature and live a transformed life.

NOTES

CHAPTER 8

THE POWER OF PRAYER

THE POWER OF PRAYER

Prayer is certainly powerful, but it's something that is not always taken seriously and often underestimated. I know that some young people don't pray, because they feel like they don't know how to pray and that their prayers won't be effective. Some have busy schedules and prayer is not always a part of it. For others, circumstances have led them to believe that God doesn't answer prayers.

Have you ever compared the way that you pray, to the way that others pray? When I was younger I would hear my parents with their powerful prayers, and go to church and hear the older saints praying prayers like, "Lord I look to thee, you are the omnipotent God. Break every chain in the mighty name of Jesus..." They were seriously going in!

I thought, "well dang! My prayers are useless, I need to pray like them." When I attempted to pray like them, it didn't sound or feel right and it even had me confused. Now that I'm older, I pray at a more mature level.

I used to think, that God was more inclined to answer those who were praying the warfare prayers and shouting at the top of their lungs, than he was to answer me. My assumption was wrong.

God's decision to answer prayers, is not based on the loudness of the prayer, or the amount of Biblical or big words used. No. It's based on the condition of your heart. You could be saying one thing with your mouth, but saying another thing in your heart.

Through prayer, you communicate with God. This can be done in many different ways. That might be praying in your heart, praying aloud or writing prayers down and reciting them etc.

Communicate with God, in the way that's comfortable to you. Jesus calls you friend, so you can simply talk to him like how you would talk to your friend. Just have a normal conversation with him.

My favourite Christian movie, which you may have heard or seen is "War Room". The movie focuses on a woman by the name of Elizabeth, whose marriage is falling apart. She just didn't know how to fix it. She meets an elderly woman who encourages her to fight for her marriage through prayer.

The "War room" is a prayer closet, and Elizabeth becomes dedicated to writing down all her prayers and praying in it – declaring the word of the Lord, taking authority over the enemy and cancelling all his plans. The scripture *1st Thessalonians 5:17* instructs us to *"pray without ceasing"*. This is precisely what Elizabeth did in *War Room*.

Prayer is the one thing that saves her marriage, and brings her family back together. God turned things around! I really thank the Lord for that movie; it was life changing for me.

In the first chapter, I mentioned that I wrote my prayers down on Notecards, well that idea was inspired by the movie. I bought a book called *"Fervent"* by Priscilla Shirer – who played the character Elizabeth in *War Room*. At the back of the book there were 10 pull-out notecards to write prayers on, which was so effective. I still go back to those prayers now.

Have you ever been frustrated because you've been praying about something and it hasn't come to pass? I've been there. I encourage you to keep praying, even if you don't see results. Don't stop praying until your breakthrough comes.

When I was younger, Facebook was my life. I used it to express my personal thoughts. There were a lot of things that I should've kept to myself. At the time, I saw nothing wrong with my Facebook statuses; I mean...The status box does ask, "What's on your mind?" So, I simply expressed what was on my mind.

I spent all that time exposing my issues to everyone, when I should've just taken it to the Lord in prayer. Thankfully, I'm not like that on Facebook anymore.

Some people on Facebook now, are just like the old me. They love to share their drama with everyone on Facebook and spill all the tea. When I see their posts, in my head I'm like "Honey nooo, why are you telling everyone your business? Tell it to Jesus!" In times of trouble you should pray. Before you tell anyone else, tell it to Jesus.

It's nice to have people to talk to, but it's very important that you talk to people who you know that you can trust. If you don't have anyone to talk to, ask God to direct you to the right people.

In *Philippians 4:6*, it says *"Do not be anxious about anything, but in every situation, by prayer and petition, with thanksgiving, present your requests to God."* When going to God in prayer, you must pray believing that God is able to answer your prayers. There is no point of praying, if you don't really believe, and you shouldn't be mad at God, if your prayers are unanswered.

From experience, I can honestly say, that there is power in prayer. God has answered many of my prayers; meeting me at the point of my needs. I have been healed, delivered, transformed, all because I prayed and people have prayed for me. The Lord heard my hearts cry.

The power of prayer is demonstrated in *1st Kings 17:21-22.* The Prophet Elijah was staying with a widow and her son. Sadly the son fell ill and died. Verse 21 says *"then he stretched himself out on the boy three times and cried out to the Lord, "Lord my God, let this boy's life return to him!"* Verse 22, "The Lord heard Elijah's cry, and the boy's life returned to him and he lived." Praise God! Due to Elijah's effective prayers, the boy who was physically dead, was resurrected.

That can still be done today, God has not changed and will never change. If you're struggling with dead situations, call upon the name of the Lord. Dead ambitions can resurrect, dead love can resurrect, dead relationships can resurrect. Dead finance can resurrect, dead faith can resurrect. Nothing is too hard for God, you just need to trust him.

In *Mark 9,* a man brought his son to Jesus, so that the boy could be healed and delivered from a spirit that tormented him and made him unable to speak. The disciples weren't able to cast out the spirit, but Jesus was. When the disciples asked Jesus why they couldn't do it, his reply was, *"This kind can come forth by nothing, but by prayer and fasting." (Mark 9:29)* Some situations won't change, until you go deep into prayer and fasting.

The scripture *1st Corinthians 14:2,* tells us, *"For he that speaketh in an unknown tongue speaketh not unto men, but unto God: for no man understandeth him; howbeit in the spirit he speaketh mysteries."* Amen.

Having the gift of speaking in tongues is important and has many benefits. These benefits include: Speaking directly to God in a heavenly language – the language that he gifted you with. Having access to revelations from God, that are hidden to others, being connected on a deeper level with God and receiving strength, power and a personal transformation.

I used to get annoyed, when the older saints would constantly tell me to seek to be filled with the Holy Ghost, and to have the evidence of speaking in tongues, but I get it now.

Prayer is our spiritual weapon, did you know that? *2nd Corinthians 10:4* – *"For the weapons of our warfare are not carnal but mighty through God, to the pulling down of strong holds."* In this spiritual warfare, your prayer is mighty through God and has the power to pull down strong holds, break every chain, release blessings and destroy the plans of the enemy!

Satan is aware of this and it scares him, so he'll do everything he can to stop you from praying. Have you been struggling with your prayer life; lacking the focus and desire to pray? Do you try to pray but end up falling asleep? During prayer time in church, is your mind elsewhere? That's the enemy distracting you, he doesn't want you to pray, because you're weak without your spiritual weapon.

If you can't stand in prayer, you will fall and be defeated. Prayer brings victory. In *2nd Chronicles 20:1-24*, King Jehoshaphat proclaimed that there would be prayer and fasting throughout all of Judah, as the Moabites and Amorite armies, were coming against him in battle. He knew that his army wasn't big enough to conquer the opposing army.

Everyone prayed diligently and worshipped, and God set people to ambush and kill the huge army. King Jehoshaphat and the whole of Judah were victorious and saved because of their prayers. God will fight your battles!

Can you imagine how incredible it would be, if this generation got serious about prayer?!! My prayer is that we will have the determination and desire to pray more. It's so important that you pray by yourself and also pray for others and with others. *"Iron sharpeneth iron" (Proverbs 27:17).*

Of course everyone prays together as a church, but it's good to have someone, or a group that you can pray with when you're not in church. That might be, meeting up with a few people from your church, or Christian friends outside of your church. I recommend that you find people that you can pray with.

There are some great Christian groups around, like the Pinky Promise group (that I'm a part of) and the Mancave Society group, founded by the U.S Power couple, Heather and Cornelius Lindsey. They have various branches, so you might be able to find a group that's close to where you live.

In these groups, you'll find people who you can talk to and pray with. The meetings that I've attended so far have left me inspired and uplifted. It's good that these Christian groups are in place and that prayer is an important aspect in them.

Prayer is needed and there is truly power in prayer.

Don't reject it and don't underestimate it. Make praying your priority.

NOTES

CHAPTER 9

DEFEATING GOLIATH

CHAPTER 9

DEFEATING GOLIATH

'Defeating Goliath' was the name of a topic that we had for a youth Sunday at my church—my personal favourite! The topic blessed me, and I just had to share my thoughts with you in this book.

So, let me get into it, In *1st Samuel 16,* God no longer wants King Saul to reign as king over Israel, due to his disobedience. God tells the prophet Samuel to go to Jesse the Bethlehemite, as the new king would be one of Jesse's sons.

Samuel obeys, and when he gets there, he sees Eliab—Jesse's eldest son. Immediately, he thinks, "Clearly, this is the guy! I've found the new King!" Samuel was looking at Eliab's physical stature, but God was looking at the heart and didn't see Eliab as the future king.

Jesse's seven sons went before Samuel, but none of them were chosen by God. So Samuel asked Jesse if they were all the children that he had. To which he replied: "There is still the youngest, he is tending the sheep". So Samuel asked Jesse to get him, and the youngest boy came.

Finally, we are introduced to David who is described as "ruddy, with bright eyes and good looking". The description of David, gives me the impression that he was a young boy; probably in his teens and the complete opposite of Eliab and his other brothers.

Despite this, God tells Samuel to *"Arise, anoint him, for this is the one!"* Wow! I'm sure David's family members were confused when he was anointed. Maybe they even questioned whether Samuel was indeed hearing from God.

They must've been thinking; "This is nonsense! David is a Shepherd boy! How can a little Shepherd boy reign as king and lead a nation?" But the Lord's ways are not our ways, neither are His thoughts our thoughts.

In the following chapter, Jesse tells David to take food for his older brothers, who were Israelite soldiers away at war with the Philistines. As David arrives and is chatting away with his brothers, he hears Goliath—a giant from the Philistine army, insulting the Israelites and demanding that a man should be sent to fight him. This was the regular occurrence for 40 days, every morning and evening.

The Bible says that whenever the Israelites saw Goliath, they "fled from him in great fear". They were petrified! It's interesting that despite them being men of war, fully armed and fully trained, one giant had the whole army paralysed in fear.

Now, David's reaction to Goliath was completely different and never fails to make me laugh. In slang terms, he said "Nahhhh! Is this a joke ting? Whooo is this Wasteman please?!
Who is this uncircumcised fool disrespecting the armies of the living God!"

David was so fearless and told King Saul that he would be the one to fight Goliath. Saul took one look at him and dismissed the idea, saying that David was too young and not strong enough to fight Goliath.

So, David started to recount to Saul about a time when a lion and bear tried to take one of his sheep away. He mentions how he chased them and rescued the sheep from their jaws by striking and killing both the lion and the bear. He was confident that Goliath would have the same fate and that God would deliver him once again.

Saul then gives David his blessing and dresses him in armour, puts a bronze helmet on his head and gives him a sword. He wanted David to be prepared for the fight. However, David decided not to fight with the armour as he wasn't used to it. Instead, he opted for a slingshot and five smooth stones that he found at a stream and went down to the battle line.

I imagine that the Israelite army burst out laughing, and hid their faces in disbelief when they saw what David did. Maybe they shouted "You are very stupid if you think that you can kill the giant with your little stones! See you in heaven mate!"

The Bible states Goliath was "*six cubits and a span. He had a bronze helmet on his head and wore a coat of scale armour of bronze weighing five thousand shekels; on his legs he wore bronze greaves and a bronze javelin was slung on his back. His spear shaft was like a weaver's rod and its iron point weighed six hundred shekels. His shield bearer went ahead of him."*

To be honest, every time I read this, I roll my eyes. Goliath was a giant, and he was heavily protected with armour. I don't understand why he needed a shield bearer in front of him...he was too extra!

From reading the description of Goliath, it would seem that David had no chance of defeating him with just a slingshot and stones. In the eyes of man, he looked foolish. *1ˢᵗ Corinthians 1: 27 tells us that "God chose what the world thinks foolish to shame the wise, and God chose what the world thinks weak to shame the strong."*

When Goliath realised that David was just a boy and only had a slingshot and stones, he mocked, cursed him and threatened him saying: "I'll give your flesh to the birds and the wild animals."

David replied, *"You come against me with sword and spear and javelin, but I come against you in the name of the Lord Almighty..."* Amen! David also declared that the Lord would deliver Goliath into his hands and that he would cut off Goliath's head etc. His closing statement was *"it is not by sword or spear that the Lord saves; for the battle is the Lord's, and he will give all of you into our hands."*

What a powerful response! What a powerful statement! The thing that stood out to me the most was David's "God-fidence", meaning his confidence in God. He didn't put his trust in his own abilities or strength, but instead, put his complete trust in the Lord.

So, back to the battle, the Bible says that as Goliath moved closer to attack David, David ran towards him. He took a stone from his bag and slung it. The stone then sunk into Goliath's forehead and he died instantly. That fight was over in a flash.

I believe that the five smooth stones that David picked up are significant because they represent JESUS. Goliath's thick armour and protection were useless and of no effect against David's stone. If the stones represent Jesus, then it shows the magnitude of power in that name. One stone was enough to bring the giant down!

All the things that David said would happen happened. God did deliver Goliath into his hands. David did strike him down and cut off his head. He wasn't just victorious because he took the Lord in battle but also because of his strong faith and ability to speak things into existence.

David is my inspiration. He was so strong-willed, yet he didn't have much of a support system and was often overlooked. His dad Jesse, didn't see a king in him. If Samuel didn't ask Jesse if he had more sons, I doubt that David would've been called to stand before him. Also, when David inquired about Goliath to some of the Israelite men, his oldest brother heard about it and got angry with him and then belittled him in front of everyone.

When David said he wanted to fight Goliath, Saul told him that he was too young and not good enough. Under all of those circumstances, some people would've called it quits.

But David wasn't fazed by the negativity of others. A lot can be learnt from him.

In *Numbers 13*, God planned to give the Israelites the land of Canaan, but told Moses to send some men to explore the land first. Moses sent twelve men out and ten of them returned with a bad report, saying that there was no way that they could take over the land. When they explored the land, they saw powerful people, fortified and large cities and giants too. They were terrified.

However, two of the men returned with a good report. Their names were Caleb and Joshua. Caleb silenced the negative men and said "We should go up and take possession of the land, for we can certainly do it."

The response of the other men was, "We can't attack those people; they are stronger than we are...we seemed like grasshoppers in our own eyes and we looked the same to them." The men saw the giants and immediately felt smaller than they actually were. They believed that it was impossible for the Israelites to take the land.

Caleb and Joshua on the other hand, saw the powerful people, the large fortified cities and the giants but they were unfazed by those things. They were not fearful. Caleb did not say that the Israelites could "possibly" take possession of the land; he said that they could "certainly do it." Caleb and Joshua knew that God was with them and if God was with them, who could be against them?!

They had strong faith, so when they saw the land, they saw an opportunity to conquer it.

Further on in the scripture, you'll see that the Israelites believed the bad report and turned against God, saying things like "Wouldn't it be better for us to go back to Egypt?"
Can you imagine! They wanted to go back to being enslaved and mistreated. That's crazy! They forgot about all the things God had done for them. They should've known that if God had delivered them before, he was more than able to deliver them again.

The Israelites made God angry, and he almost destroys them but Moses pleaded with God to have mercy on them. God punished the Israelites instead, by not allowing them to enter into the promised land. They missed out on their blessing. As Caleb and Joshua had faith in God and followed him wholeheartedly, God brought them both into the promised land.

When you go through rough situations and trials, it may seem like your back is against the wall and all hope is lost. Don't be like the Israelites and turn against God, forgetting where he has brought you from. Remember that the Lord is with you and is able to deliver you.

Just like Caleb, silence those negative people and negative thoughts and increase your faith. God has given you the power to defeat Goliath. However, if you fail to realise that and live in fear, Goliath will defeat you and you'll miss out on some of God's blessings for you.

PURPOSE

Goliath represents the physical, mental and spiritual stumbling blocks that we encounter in life. Goliath for me, has been my emotions and suppressing them. Sometimes deep down I'm sad, but I put on a mask to hide my true feelings from others.

The reason why I do that, is because I want people to see me as someone who is happy, confident and strong but it's hard to keep the mask on. There have been times where I've just burst into tears, unable to contain my emotions. It's not good to keep everything in and it can definitely take a toll on your health. So I'm going to stop suppressing my feelings so much and I choose to be positive. Goliath is defeated!

Another Goliath for me was fear; for most of my life, I was afraid. Afraid to talk to people, afraid to stand before people, afraid to step out of my comfort zone, afraid to open up, afraid to operate in my gifts, etc.

Fear held me back from making progress. There were so many things that I should've done, but couldn't bring myself to do. I Thank God because a few years ago, I bought a book by Joyce Meyer called "Battlefield of the mind". Incredible book!

In the book, Joyce Meyer talks about how the spirit of fear is a type of Goliath. The two quotes of hers that stood out to me the most were: *"If you're too afraid to do it, do it afraid!"* and *"Giants only fall when you face them."* These quotes changed my life!

I realised that the reason I was struggling with fear for so long, was because I was too afraid to face my fears. All I ever did was run away from them. I was determined to change, and with that realisation, I decided to put myself in situations where I had no choice but to face my fears.

I started performing at open mic nights, singing in front of small and large audiences. I also performed Spoken Word and recently went to a Public speaking workshop. I did so many things that were out of my comfort zone. Was I afraid to do those things? YES! But I did them anyway; I did them afraid!

I found that the more that I pushed myself, the further I grew in confidence. The more I faced the giant; the further I became victorious. I am now confidently contributing in discussions; I am making more of an effort to talk to others and making new friends in the process and I enjoy standing in front of people to speak now.

Some months ago, I joined a six week programme called Spear. The programme is for young people aged 16-24 that are unemployed and not in education. The Spear coaches help young people to overcome the barriers that prevent them from getting into work, or in the place where they want to be in life and also help to guide them in the right direction.

It includes training on how to deliver great presentations, how to write a great CV, mock interviews etc. I loved it! I gained a lot more confidence from being on the programme and I'm so happy that I had the courage to be a part of it.

At the end of the program, there is a celebration evening,

where all the young people have to give a presentation about their journey and where they are now. I feared that my presentation wouldn't flow well and that I would forget to address the key points. Nonetheless, I kept practicing what I would say and remained positive and confident about it.

When the day finally came for me to do my presentation, I stood up with confidence and delivered an excellent well structured presentation. It flowed well and I remembered all the key points and more. I am a great speaker! Don't let fear stop you from achieving greatness!

Your Goliath may be fear as well, or it may be insecurities, anger, bitterness, addictions, relationships, sleeping around, lack of self-control, etc. Do not let the giants win! Just like David ran towards Goliath, face the issues!

Maybe you're someone who has experienced being overlooked and overshadowed, like myself. Maybe people have drowned you in limitations; telling you that you're too young to do this, you're not qualified to do that, your time has passed, you're not smart enough, you're not pretty enough or handsome enough, you're not strong enough.

Rise above the limitations! Don't disqualify yourself and self-sabotage. Remember that in Christ you are more than a conqueror. Greater is he that is in you, than he that is in the world. - 1st John 4:4.

It doesn't matter how long you've been struggling. It doesn't matter how big you think your Goliath is. I can assure you that nothing is too hard for God!

I also want you to know and remember, that although you live in a microwave generation, you can't always expect microwave results from God. God works in His own time, but He's always on time. He is intentional. He is Jehovah Rapha—the Lord who heals; He is Jehovah Jireh—your provider.

Do not allow others to limit you! Do not limit yourself and your abilities! And most importantly, do not limit God!

NOTES

CHAPTER 10

PROGRESS IS A PROCESS

CHAPTER 10

PROGRESS IS A PROCESS

Have you ever felt inadequate? Are you frustrated because you feel like you haven't made much progress? Do you feel like you're not where you should be in life? I know these feelings all too well.

There was a time when my voice was rarely heard. Some people even wondered if I could speak. I wanted to talk more, but I was always scared that I would say the wrong things and embarrass myself and sometimes the words just didn't come to me. Also, many times when I tried to speak up, people would cut me off or talk over me. I felt like there was no point in even trying.

Whenever I got invited to meetups and events, I would often find an excuse not to go. I'm sure that when the meetings were arranged, everyone else said, "This is gonna be LIT!", "I can't wait to see everyone." These times, my thoughts were, "I can't go, I'm socially awkward." "I'm irrelevant; they won't miss me if I'm not there." When I didn't go, I would hear everyone going on about how much fun they had. I hated that I missed out.

Most people made the assumption that I was okay and that I just didn't want to hang around them and would rather be somewhere else. In actuality, I wanted to be around them but was just really struggling to do so.

Don't just assume things about people, because you never know what people are going through.

Mahatma Ghandi said *"Be the change that you wish to see in the world."* I personalized that quote and changed it to *"Become the change that you wish to see in yourself."* I desperately wanted to see a change in myself, and repeating that statement, gave me the motivation to push myself more.

One of my goals for the beginning of last year was to lead a youth service at my church. I shared this with my youth group, and my youth leader gave me the approval to lead.

So on February 19, 2017, I led my first Youth service! As the time drew near for me to lead, I became extremely nervous but I encouraged myself with God's word and began to tell myself, "I am more than a conqueror" "I can do all things through Christ that strengthens me." Repeating those words gave me peace of mind. I reminded myself that I had to accomplish my goal. I had to make progress.

When I finally stood behind the pulpit to lead, I didn't feel afraid. I felt so comfortable and confident. I led the service really well, and the church brethren told me that it was such a blessing and they loved the way that I lead it.

Someone told me, that it looked like I had been leading services for years. One of the pastors even said he was amazed, that I was able to lead the service with such confidence.

I thank God!

Imagine if I let fear get the better of me and changed my mind about leading the service. I would not have known that I had the ability to lead. Now, I love being behind the pulpit and actually want to be called up to minister.

I now introduce myself to others and start conversations, I do presentations with a lot more boldness and I'm socializing more. It's amazing to see how much I've grown in confidence. I had to really push myself to get here and I'm so thankful for the amount of progress that I've made and will continue to make. I've been able to see my progress because I didn't give up in the process!

I encourage you also, to celebrate even the smallest achievements. This is something that I've been doing. Acknowledge and appreciate your achievements. You may have set a goal, but only managed to do a few things towards achieving it. Instead of feeling sorry for yourself, celebrate the fact that you are a step closer to achieving that goal.

In this generation of "quick fixes"—the microwave generation, when things don't happen instantly, people get upset. They want to see progress without going through the process.

It's in your process that God shapes and prepares you for who you are called to be. (Hebrews 10:36 – You need to persevere so that when you have done the will of God, you will *receive what he has promised.)*

I'll be totally honest with you; the process doesn't always feel good; it hurts sometimes. Sometimes, the process requires you to let go of things in your life that are familiar and comfortable to you. You might need to let go of certain friends and distance yourself from certain people.

In the process, you might experience loneliness and feel like God has forgotten you, but know that He will never leave you nor forsake you. I used to think that God had forgotten about me; I felt stagnant and saw everyone else moving forward and doing great things with their lives.

My problem was that I was so focused on what everyone else was doing and not actually doing anything myself. You have to make a move! Don't complain that you do not see a change in your life, when it's you who is not willing to put in the work.

Also, don't be so wrapped up in the lives of others, comparing their stage in life to yours. There are levels to this! Maybe you're supposed to be in the same position as someone else, and maybe you know it, but not everyone will be at the same stage, at the same time.

Your journey is most likely to be different from others. It may take you longer to get to where you're supposed to be, but remain faithful on the journey. God's timing is best and His timing is right.

Furthermore, don't let anyone stop you from believing that

your progress is possible. If anyone tells you, or has told you in the past that you are incapable of changing, don't accept it. They are not God! God has a plan for your life. He sees great potential in you and has created you with purpose. So, hold on!

Below are some examples of famous people, who experienced various setbacks and failure in their lives. However, they worked hard and eventually became success stories.

Tori Kelly

In 2010, she auditioned for American Idol and received harsh criticism from Simon Cowell. Kelly made it through but failed to make it into the Top 24. She continued to pursue her dreams and worked on her own music. In 2012, Kelly released her very first EP called *Handmade Songs by Tori Kelly;* which she wrote and self-produced. The following year she got signed by a record label and now has a successful music career. She's been #1 on Billboards, nominated for Grammys, and has won various awards. She also voiced the character Meena, from the successful animation film *Sing.*

Sidney Poitier

Poitier auditioned to be an actor for the North American Negro Theatre, but was rejected because of his Bahamian accent and poor reading skills. He decided to work as a dishwasher and his

Co-worker helped him to improve with his reading. Poitier also worked hard to change his accent by listening to the radio. Six months later, he returned to the theatre and was accepted. Poitier became the first black man to win an Oscar.

Oprah Winfrey
She was fired from her first job on television because she was believed to be "unfit for TV". She was devastated but didn't give up. Years later she had her own show, "The Oprah Winfrey Show" which was one of the highest ranking shows in America and she's had even greater success.

Thomas Edison
As an inventor, he failed to invent the light bulb 1,000 times. Many people probably would've given up, but he refused to give up and on his 1,001 attempt he was successful.

These people all realised, that in order to achieve great success, they needed to have endurance and perseverance. If you fail you can succeed! Trust Jesus and persevere, Progress is a process!

NOTES

CHAPTER 11

STOP SLEEPING ON YOUR GIFTS

CHAPTER 11

STOP SLEEPING ON YOUR GIFTS

James 1:17 says that *"every good gift and every perfect gift is from above"*. God created everyone with gifts and blessed you with yours for a reason.

If you have no idea what your gifting area is, seek the Lord diligently and He will make it clear unto you. I heard this awesome quote by Steve Harvey a while back; he said: "Your gift is the thing you do the best with the least amount of effort." I love this quote, and for the most part, I agree with it.

I know that I'm gifted to sing because singing is something that I do the best with the least amount of effort. I know that I'm gifted to write, as I've been passionate about writing since I was a little girl. Teachers were always impressed with my ability to construct words, sentences and ideas together.

My mum told me a few years ago, that when I was in Primary school, she went to my parents evening and my teacher said, "I won't be surprised if Lydia ends up writing a book one day." Years later and here I am, with my first book! That is so incredible to me. Look at God!

"Do not despise these small beginnings" – Zechariah 4:10 . You have to start from somewhere. You'll be surprised what God can do with a gift that you think is "small".

PURPOSE

I believe that there are specific gifts assigned to everyone for a specific purpose. Even if you have the same gift as someone else, the way you operate in that gift is most likely to be different from the other person.

In *Romans 12:6,* it clearly states that by His grace, God has given different gifts to each individual person. Examples of some of the gifts listed in verses 6 to 8 are prophecy, ministry, teaching, etc. There are so many gifts that God has graced us with, and every single gift is necessary.

Sadly, there are some people who are discontent with the gifts that God has given to them. I remember hearing a young woman say, "All I do is encourage people, it's not anything big." She believed that her gift was small and insignificant when in actuality, her gift is substantial.

A person who has the gift of encouraging others, knows the right words to say and when to say them. They are able to give wise counsel to those in need of it and uplift them. Not everyone is effective in doing that, and I know that many lives have been transformed and saved as a result of being encouraged.

We must appreciate the gifts that God has blessed us with and use them to bless others. In *Matthew 25*, Jesus teaches His disciples with the parable of the talents. The parable is about a man who was travelling and gave three of his servants talents based on their abilities.

One was given five talents, one was given two talents, and the other was given one talent. The servant with five talents traded his and gained five more. The servant with two talents did the same and received two more. However, the servant with one talent decided not to do anything with his and hid his talent.

When their master returned, inquiring about how the servants used their talents, the two servants who traded their talents and gained more, revealed it to their master. He was so pleased, his response was, "Well done, my good and faithful servant. You have been faithful over a few things, I will make you ruler over many things. Enter into the joy of your Lord." What a wonderful thing to hear. They even got more blessings. You reap what you sow.

Now, when the other servant revealed that he hid his talent, the master was very angry with him and punished him by taking his talent away and giving it to the servant with 10 talents. That's actually so sad. The other two servants could celebrate and sing: "Everything na double double O" and the poor guy couldn't even relate. I know he felt shame!

The master in this parable represents God. When God gives you a gift, He expects you to use it. If you neglect your gift, it's of no effect.

I think as young people; we tend to sometimes have the mindset of, "There will always be other times". Listen, tomorrow is not promised. If God has the power to give gifts, then He also has the power to take them away, if you chose not to use them.

Maybe you're afraid of using your gifts, as using them might mean stepping out of your comfort zone, or you're worried about what people will say. Rebuke that spirit of fear!

If you feel like there have been no opportunities for you to utilize your gifts, then maybe it's time for you to be bold and create opportunities for yourself.

Don't underestimate yourself. God entrusted you with the Gift, because He knew you had the ability to handle it. He wants to take you higher, but if you remain fearful, you'll miss your season of elevation.

Don't be so concerned about the opinions of others. There are many haters around, but you should never allow them to get the better of you. Love YOU. Be YOU. Do YOU! Regardless of what people may say or think of you. Love yourself, be yourself and do what you want to do and what you've been called to do.

Don't let anyone stop you from using your gifts, *Proverbs 18:16* reads, *"Your gift will make room for you and bring you before great men."* When you exercise your gifts, doors will start to open for you. You'll experience greater achievements in your life, and if used effectively, your gifts will also help you to connect with the right people as well. Cultivate your gifts!

Your gifts are also needed to build up your ministry and edify the church. If you're gifted to lead, lead! If you're gifted to sing, sing! If you're gifted to teach, teach! If you're gifted to preach, preach! If you're a gifted musician, play your instrument!

You never know who your gift will bless. If you don't use your gifts, then you'll rob someone of their blessing.

My dad made a powerful statement one time; he said: "The world may not read the Bible, but they read you." Amen! When people see you using your God-given gifts and growing in them, it might be the very thing that inspires and convicts them to get to know Jesus.

For some people, it may even cause them to return to the faith. I'm sure by now; you understand how important it is not to sleep on your gifts. So, keep praying to God for revelation and elevation in regards to your gifting area.

My prayer is that from reading this, you will have the boldness and desire to operate in your gifts and exceed in doing it.

NOTES

CHAPTER 12

"WOKE" CHRISTIAN

CHAPTER 12

"WOKE" CHRISTIAN

I'm sure you've heard of the term being "WOKE". A person who is *woke* is aware of social and racial issues and the injustice in the world. It's good to be aware of current affairs and not turn a blind eye to them.

So what does it mean to be a Woke Christian? To me, the term is a double entendre. It can mean being a Christian who is aware of the issues in society and around the world. (Some Christians choose not to be informed about those things.)

It can also mean, a Christian who studies the scriptures for themselves and has a clearer understanding of the word. They realise the importance of being the change and influencing change. They are radical; thinking outside the box and finding distinctive ways of witnessing to others.

I want to focus on the latter. We are the Woke generation! We are no longer taking information at face value but looking deeper into the information or teachings that we've been given.

There is a popular scripture that you may be familiar with; it's *Romans 12:2,* which says *"be not conformed to this world: but be ye transformed by the renewing of your mind."* It's a clear command for us not to be "worldly".

The dictionary definition of *worldly* is to be "concerned with material values or ordinary life rather than a spiritual existence". So basically, it's living a life that is not in line with Godly principles.

In the Bible, you'll find a great deal on modesty and how a Christian should present themselves. I just feel like some people are way too deep and blow things way out of proportion. For example, some people act like it's a sin for a boy to have a stylish haircut. I don't get it.

For Christian women, issues sometimes arise in the way that we choose to style our hair. This brings me to my next scripture, *1st Peter 3:3-4 – "Your beauty should not come from outward adornment, such as elaborate hairstyles and the wearing of gold jewellery or fine clothes. Rather, it should be that of your inner self, the unfading beauty of a gentle and quiet spirit, which is of great worth in God's sight."*

This scripture is a teaching on how wives should act and present themselves. However, I believe it's relatable to both young men and women. You shouldn't try to make yourself look more beautiful or handsome for attention or status; instead, your beauty should come from within.

I met this man once who believed that it was a sin for women to comb their hair and do anything to their hair. He probably got that idea from the scripture above, but that's wrong. Women should look presentable and take care of themselves; likewise, men should also, just not to the point of becoming vain and doing the most.

So, moving on to the popular topic of clothing, modesty is something that is important for us to take heed to. You should wear appropriate clothing that isn't a distraction and a stumbling block for others.

Dressing modestly and appropriately is not something that should be overlooked, but *1ˢᵗ Samuel 16:7* says *"people look at the outward appearance, but the Lord looks at the heart"*.
Our heart is what God is most concerned about.
Is your heart right with God?

Jesus is coming back very soon; I know that it sounds like a broken record, but it's the truth. All the signs are there. Will you make it to heaven? I've achieved many things in my life, but have I done enough for the kingdom? I don't think so. Now and again, I post empowering scriptures and words of encouragement on Social media, but I know that I should be doing more. I'm praying for the boldness to do more.

God instructs us to *"Go into all the world and proclaim the gospel to the whole creation" (Mark 16:15)*. I need to be a witness; you need to be a witness. We need to be a light for our generation. There are so many young people who don't know Jesus for themselves and don't go to church. Ask yourself the question: What can I do to help bring them in? How can I connect with them?

Handing out tracks to people is a very common method of witnessing. I'm not knocking that method, I just think that other approaches should be used in order to attract young people.

Maybe there are some young people who would like to go to church but feel like church people don't relate to them. This is why it's important to share your testimony with others; tell other young people about what Jesus has done for you. When you open up and share your story, they will probably be more inclined to listen and may open up also.

There are some Christians that I know, whose whole life revolves around church. Church is all they know. When they text me, it's always some long essay about Bible scriptures, videos of people talking about God, or an invitation to their church Bible study. It's great that they love the Lord, but a "Hello" would be nice. A "how are you?" would be great. It makes me not want to respond to them, and many times I don't.

I think for someone who doesn't go to church or have a personal relationship with Jesus, it might be better to approach them on their level. Find a common interest between you and them.

For example, I really love music and I'm eclectic in regards to the types of music that I listen to. I'm aware of the current secular artists. I also listen to and know many Gospel songs. There are actually different genres within Gospel music and I love that! If I met someone who was into rap music, I could then introduce them to Gospel rap music. If I met someone who was into Neo-soul, I could introduce them to some great Gospel Neo-soul music etc.

In *1ˢᵗ Corinthians 9:19-23,* the Apostle Paul talks about being all things to all people, so that more people can be saved. If all you know is church, how do you expect to reach other young people who have been brought up in a different environment? Jesus was out of the box when it came to winning souls for the kingdom, and we should also be.

The Apostle Paul was WOKE, in the sense that he recognised that in order to reach the people and win souls, he had to meet them at their level. That doesn't mean you should follow people in sin, not at all! It just makes a difference when you're relatable.

My youth leader is great at putting on events and organised an event called "Aim Higher". It was open to the public, and she brought in successful young people; entrepreneurs, motivational speakers, authors, etc. I left that event so inspired and I know I wasn't the only one.

If organising events is your strength, go for it! Get people to support you in the process. If organising events is not your strength, but you have great ideas, don't keep them to yourself; share your ideas. Souls need to be saved. Young people need to be saved.

If you want to see a change, become the change that you want to see. Be proactive. You are the future! God has given you the power to influence change, so influence change.
Be WOKE. Stay WOKE!

NOTES

CHAPTER 13

YOU ARE PREDESTINED WITH PURPOSE

CHAPTER 13

YOU ARE PREDESTINED WITH PURPOSE

I feel like it only makes sense that I end with this chapter, I feel strongly inclined to do so. I want you to know with a surety that you ARE predestined with purpose.

In *Jeremiah 1:5* God says *"Before I formed you in the womb I knew you; and before you were born, I set you apart"* In *Romans 8:30*, the verse says *"those he predestined he also called, those he called he also justified, those he justified he also glorified."* Amen!

Every single person on this earth was created with a specific purpose. Sadly, not everyone is aware of what their purpose is. Many young people are okay with living a purposeless life.

For some, it's a case of laziness or feeling worthless. Others are aware of what they are called to do, but fear prevents them from pursuing it. Also, certain people lack the personal drive, which they need to change their lives. Maybe you fall into one of these categories.

There is a fascinating statement made by the late Myles Munroe, he said *"The greatest tragedy in life is not death, but a life without a purpose."* I absolutely agree with him! That would be such a waste of a life. My desire is to live the life that God predestined for me. I pray that this will be your desire also.

A prominent man in the Bible that is perfect for this chapter, is Joseph. There are great lessons to be learned from the account of his life. I'm sure you are familiar with the story of Joseph, but I'll go through it anyway.

So Joseph had 11 brothers, 10 of his brothers were very jealous of him and hated him because he was their father's favourite son. To make matters worse, Joseph had dreams and would reveal them to his brothers.

Joseph dreamt that he and his brothers were binding sheaves in the field, and all of their sheaves bowed down to his sheave. He also had another dream where he explains that the sun, moon and 11 stars "made obeisance" to him. The word obeisance means to show respect or reverence. This made the brothers hate him even more.

When Joseph went to check up on his brothers one day, they seized the perfect opportunity to get rid of him for good. They sold Joseph for 20 pieces of silver, to a group of Merchants, who were on their way to Egypt.

At the tender age of 17, Joseph's life takes a dramatic turn. He is stripped from his place of comfort and security, his father's love, his home, his livelihood, his family, everything that he is accustomed to is taken away from him. He goes from living a life of freedom to being enslaved.

Joseph becomes a servant to Potiphar (the right hand man of Pharaoh the king) and because of his great character and abilities, Potiphar promotes him to overseer of his house – huge responsibility!

Now Joseph caught the eye of Potiphar's wife, and she asks him to sleep with her. Joseph consistently resisted her advances and one day when he resisted she grabbed his robe. Joseph ran away leaving her with the robe in her hand.

He ends up being falsely accused of rape and then imprisoned. Even in prison though, the Bible says that the Lord was with Joseph.

It's in prison, that God blesses Joseph with the gift of interpreting dreams. He interprets the dreams of the king's Chief Butler and Baker; revealing to the Chief Butler, that in three days he would be restored to his previous position in the King's house. Joseph asked the Butler to remember him when it happens, but he forgot all about Joseph.

Two years later, Pharaoh has a dream that troubles him. He calls on all the magicians and wise men of the land, but none of them are able to interpret the dream. The Chief Butler finally remembered Joseph, and Joseph was brought before Pharaoh.

Joseph interprets the dream explaining to Pharaoh that there will be 7 years of plenty in Egypt, but followed by 7 years of famine. He comes up with the brilliant idea of getting people to store food away, in preparation for the famine.

Amazed at the gift and wisdom of Joseph, Pharaoh promotes him. Joseph went from being a prisoner to the ruler of a nation!

It's here, that we begin to see his purpose unfolding. Crowds from all over, travelled to Egypt to buy corn from Joseph. It so happened, that Joseph's brothers also travelled to buy corn from the ruler of Egypt.

They were completely oblivious to the fact that the ruler of Egypt, was none other than their baby brother. The one that they hated and sold into slavery. As soon as the brothers see Joseph, what do they do? Well...They bow!

BOOM!

Joseph recognised them instantly, remembering the dreams that he had as a young boy.

The author Mark Twain said, *"The two most important days in your life, are the day you were born and the day you find out why."* Joseph discovered why he was born. He realised that the dreams were a foreshadowing of his destiny. In that moment, Joseph experiences the fulfillment of his destiny. I get chills every time!

He tried his best to hide his true identity, but loses his composure and eventually breaks down, revealing himself to his brothers. There was no hatred, bitterness or anger in his heart at all, only love. Joseph then goes on to bless his entire family with a great deal of, riches, food, land etc.

It's so ironic, that the one that the brothers wanted out of their lives, the one that they wanted dead, was ultimately the chosen one to save them. The story of Joseph is so encouraging and inspiring to me.

Joseph's life was a Rollercoaster, but even in his darkest hour, he kept the faith and put his trust in the Lord, despite not knowing when his change would come. It was clear that God was faithful to Joseph, as he was constantly coming through for him and proved that he was always in control. God makes no mistakes!

Just like Joseph was taken out of his comfort zone, and had to endure hard trials, before seeing his purpose fulfilled, God might have to remove you from your place of comfort to put you on the road to purpose.

The Lord is the potter, and we are the clay. Sometimes, He has to break us down, rebuild and shape us into who He wants us to be. This won't always feel good, but it will work out for your good.

If you don't know what your purpose is in life, Jesus says in *Matthew 6:33*, *"Seek ye first the kingdom of God, and his righteousness and all these things shall be added unto you."* You must stay consistent in prayer and seek God. God speaks and directs, but you have to make yourself available to receive from Him.

Remove yourself from distractions, and spend quality time with God. The more you draw close to God, the further He will draw close to you.

Also, I know it can be so frustrating when you are seeking the Lord for clarity on your purpose but not receiving any confirmation from Him. Please, don't give up on God! Remember that the Lord doesn't always come right away, but He's always right on time.

You could even get people to pray with you and for you, in regards to you discovering your purpose. (e.g., Church leaders, church family, friends, etc.) You never know, God might choose not to reveal your purpose directly to you but to someone else on your behalf. He works in mysterious ways.

Often, the thing that hinders some people from knowing their distinct calling is the fact that they are pursuing a purpose that doesn't belong to them. I watched a YouTube video some years ago where Steve Harvey was on TBN teaching on the pursuit of passion in comparison to the quest for purpose.

He explained that there are some people who devote their life to pursuing what they are passionate about, believing that their passion is the thing that they were destined to do. The problem is, passion is not always a direct link to purpose.

Some auditionees on XFactor, are prime examples of this. They will come on stage talking about how they can sing as good as Whitney Houston, Mariah Carey or Michael Jackson (I immediately prepare for the worst). Some even have the audacity to say that they can sing better than them.

When they finally start singing now, their voice is DEAD! Absolutely awful! Those people are passionate about singing, but singing is clearly not their calling. They are just not musically inclined and that's okay, I mean...it's not for everyone. Maybe they are better artists, or destined to be teachers or councilors, but because they pursue passion, it hinders them from realising this.

There are certain people that you will find in the secular world, and even in the church, who are envious of the position of others an want to take over from them. This takeover spirit is wrong, because it prevents others from growing and growth is necessary.

Those that choose to take over a certain area or department, will find that they struggle with progression. Whereas another person will come and do the exact same thing as them, and have no issues and more success.

The reason being that they are pursuing something that God hasn't given them the grace to do. Myles Munroe said it best, "Provision isn't there unless the vision is yours" Ask Jesus to show you what it is that you should be doing. When you walk in line with your purpose, provision will be yours. You'll see the Lord enlarge your territory. God can't supply you with what does not belong to you.

I just want to encourage you, to not give up on your purpose. Maybe you're in a situation, where your friends and those around you know theirs, and you feel lost as you have no idea what your purpose is.

My friend, that does not mean that you were created without purpose. God did not forget about you, you are fearfully and wonderfully made. That means a lot of thought and care went into creating you.

If you even look at the creation of the world; the sun, moon, stars, trees, birds and other living things, were all created for a precise reason and with an established role. How much more you, who was made in the image and likeness of the Almighty God?!

PURPOSE

Jeremiah 29:11 — "For I know the plans I have for you, plans to prosper you and not to harm you. Plans to give you hope and a future."

Purpose resides in you, but again, to find it you must seek your creator diligently. The Bible says *"ask and it shall be given unto you, seek and you will find, knock and the door shall be opened unto you."* The Lord wants to reveal things to you, but first you need to ask him, seek him and knock on the doors of his heart.

Having and knowing purpose is a blessing, but it doesn't come without its share of challenges. There are so many underlying factors, which can often get in the way of you living a purposeful life. For example, fear and doubt; I can't tell you the amount of times I've doubted myself and considered giving up on this book.

I've had a few bad experiences in the past, where I've shared ideas with others, and my ideas have been ignored. There was such a lack of support. This led me to think that there would be no support for this book. I feared that no one would want to read it and all the time and energy spent on it, would all be in vain.

Fear is the enemy of progress! Do not let the enemy win! My advice to you in regards to this, is to ask God to renew your mind, so that your thoughts will be positive. A changed mind equates to a changed life.

I want you to know, that you were blessed to be a blessing. Someone needs you to walk in purpose. Someone needs you to fulfill purpose. During this writing process, I kept telling myself, "Someone needs to read this book." "Someone's life will be changed from reading this book." It gave me the drive to keep writing.

Other factors that affect purpose, are the haters and negative people. In walking in purpose, you might experience people who constantly feel the need to kill your vibe. My next advice to you will be, know who to share things with. Not everyone will be down with your purpose honey. (If everyone is, Praise the Lord, what a blessing).

Not everyone are dream chasers. Some people don't have any aspirations or dreams of their own, so they become dream killers to those around them. The more you listen and accept the negative words that they say, is the more that you will doubt the call on your life.

The devil is a liar! When he attacks, use the word of God and say, "If God is for me who can be against me." Do not let the devil steal your joy and do not let him rewrite your story.

In the past, it's sad to say, but I've had moments where I've questioned whether my life is worth living. God's word was and still is my strength and comfort and reminded me that I have so much to live for. I want you to know that your life means something. As long as your heart beats, it's an indication of purpose.

A few months ago, I watched an incredible sermon by Pastor Michael Todd called "Marked". If you haven't seen it already, you can find it on YouTube. In the sermon, he was preaching that regardless of your situation or condition, you are marked by God!

PURPOSE

Life may not be going the way you planned for it to go but YOU are marked by God!

As I bring this chapter to a close, my prayer as mentioned before, is that you will make the decision to truly live a purposeful life and reap the benefits of this decision.

Always remember that YOU are a child of the most high God, YOU have been predestined with purpose and YOU are destined for greatness!

NOTES

I'm a 23 year old from North London, and I grew up in church. There were some things that I didn't like, but I'm grateful for my upbringing. Some of the things which were instilled in me at a young age, helped to shape me into the woman I am today.

Special shout out to my Parents and Grandparents. They raised me right and I love and appreciate them! They taught me the importance of knowing Jesus for myself and I'm glad that I do.

Although I'm passionate about music, writing has a special place in my heart. This is the first time I've written a book, but I've always been a writer. Where I struggled to express myself verbally, I was able to express myself through writing, and I put my heart onto paper.

This book is a huge achievement for me and it's such an incredible feeling to be an Author. I desire to be used by God, to make an impact and leave a legacy behind. I pray that I've done that justice with this book.

Thank you so much again for reading my book, it means a lot to me. If you would like to get in touch with me, my contact information and Social media handles are below:

EMAIL: lydia.marshall@outlook.com

FACEBOOK: Marie Marshall

INSTAGRAM: lydiamarshall62

TWITTER: @Lydzz17

LINKEDIN: Lydia Marshall

BLOG: mariespassion.wordpress.com

31840162R00082

Printed in Poland
by Amazon Fulfillment
Poland Sp. z o.o., Wrocław